Bit, But Not Poisoned

Third Printing 2006

Unless otherwise noted, all scripture quotations are taken from the King James Version of the Bible.

Scripture quotations marked (AMP) are taken from the Holy Bible, Amplified. Old Testament copyright © 1965, 1987 by The Zondervan Corporation, Grand Rapids, Michigan. The Amplified New Testament copyright © 1954, 1958, 1987 by The Lockman Foundation. Used by permission.

Scripture quotations marked (NIV) are taken from the Holy Bible, New International Version. NIV Copyright © 1973, 1978, 1984 by International Bible Society. Used by permission by Zondervan. All rights reserved.

Copyright © 1999, 2003 by Dr. Robbi Warren. All rights reserved. No part of this book may be used or reproduced in any manner whatsoever without written permission of the publisher, except in the case of brief quotations in articles and reviews. For more information write: Robbi Warren International Ministries, P.O. Box 11951, Baltimore, MD 21207-0951.

Printed in the United States of America

ISBN 1-57558-132-9

Bit, But Not Poisoned

Dr. Robbi Warren

Acknowledgements

I give praise, honor and glory to my Lord and Savior Jesus Christ who has graced me through my bites — not to be poisoned.

Tina and Danielle, thanks for allowing me to come into your lives for a season. It was during that time that God began to bring this book together. Had it not been for your long hours of transcribing, this book wouldn't have come to fruition. Love you both forever.

To my faithful right hand, Tonya, thanks for putting up with me. I know it's not easy sometimes, but your reward will be great in heaven. Love you with my life.

To my co-editor and proofreader. God knew that the baby (book) was at birth and didn't have enough strength to come forth—then came you. Tangy, words cannot express my appreciation and love for you. The time that you've given to help deliver this message of hope can only be rewarded by the Master. My prayer is that God will catapult you into a life of supernatural blessing.

To Pastor Larry Baylor, thanks for being a spiritual mentor. Your words of wisdom, prayer, and instruction have inspired me more than you will ever know.

Thanks to Dr. Jimmy Thompson, Vince Thompson and Faith Printing for supporting the vision God has given to me.

Thanks to my "Big Sis" Dr. Wanda A. Turner for all the words of encouragement you've given through the years.

Contents

Chapter One
Paul Was Bitten But Not Poisoned 15

Chapter Two
Bit by Religion 31

Chapter Three
Bit by Inferiority 43

Chapter Four
Bit by Failure 53

Chapter Five
Bit by Success 61

Chapter Six
Bit by Disease 71

Chapter Seven
Bit by Relationships 83

Chapter Eight
Bit by Infidelity and Divorce 97

Chapter Nine
Bit by Deceit 107

Chapter Ten
Bit by Bad Choices 119

Conclusion
Bit, But Not Poisoned 131

Foreword
By Dr. Wanda A. Turner

I have had the distinct pleasure of knowing Dr. Robbi Warren, author of **"Bit But Not Poisoned"** for over fifteen years. During this span of time, we have fellowshipped over the telephone, hugged at airports and even waved at one another when scheduled to minister at the same conferences. I look back over the years and think most about the wonderful, biblical truths he and I have shared and the personal testimonies of survival and victory.

Perhaps, however, the greatest truth Dr. Warren has shared with me is that which God spoke to him one day during a special time of prayer. As a traveling minister you can't help but run across a myriad of people with many problems, challenges and crisis. It often becomes the task of the visiting minister to share the healing Word of Jesus Christ to counter attack the awful assaults of satan against believers. God ministered a simple, yet powerful revelation to Dr. Warren that addresses the issues of pain, agony and trauma. Dr. Warren told me the Lord spoke to him and said, *"It's not the bite that destroys or kills, but it's the poison that comes with the bite."* Little did I know that this truth would be developed into the book you're holding right now.

I look around the body of Christ and I observe many that tell us 'what God says'. But there are only a select few that tell us 'what God means'. Dr. Robbi Warren is such a person. As I think of this book, I recall a story told to me several years ago. Perhaps you've heard or read the same tale.

A farmer taking a walk one day, stumbled across
A snake that was bleeding and laying quite limp.
The caring farmer picked up the
Snake and when he realized that the snake was still alive,
He took it home to nurse it back to health.
A few weeks later, the snake was healthy and ready to crawl and
Slither across the floors of the farmer's home.
The farmer decided to test the snake's health by taking him for
A walk on the country road.

*A few minutes into the walk, the farmer placed the
Snake close to his heart and began telling him how he enjoyed
Nursing and feeding the wounded snake.
Before he could finish talking to the snake,
The snake's tongue reached out and bit the farmer leaving its
Venomous poison in the man's system.
As the farmer began gasping for air and breathing his last breath…
He looked at the snake and asked, "Why did you bite the one helping
you?"
The snake replied, "Because that's what snakes do!"*

Too many believers in the body of Christ waste time and energy rehearsing episodes, crisis and seasons in our lives when loved ones, relatives, friends, associates and even enemies have poisoned our minds, emotions, souls, bodies and spirits with venoms such as jealousy, anger, wrath, spite, intimidation, fear and strife.

We've spent so much time and energy focusing on the deadly "bites of life" that we're too exhausted to explore the spiritual antidotes that Jesus Christ and His Word have made available to each of us in the Kingdom against the assaults of satan.

I also thought about a proverb shared by the late Bishop Wayne S. Davis in 1981. While teaching Bible Study he stated, "You can not stop a bird from flying over your head, but you can prevent it from building a nest in your hair". That's exactly what Dr. Warren's book is all about. In this book from front to back cover he will discuss the various bites we receive and then give us truth, wisdom and understanding how to prevent becoming poisoned by the bites.

Don't put this book down until you have found the answers you need for your own life. I salute Dr. Warren and encourage each of you to understand you may be **Bit, but don't become Poisoned.**

> Dr. Wanda A. Turner,
> *Pastor, Author, Prophetic Evangelist*
> *and Entrepreneur*

From the Heart of the Author

Through many years of ministering across this nation, I've encountered thousands of people who have been devastated (bitten) by life's traumas. For some, the hurt has been so tangible that they've come to despise life and lose hope. In my quest to offer consolation to them, the Lord caused me to reflect on my own personal struggles; and so I find that often the true place of effective ministry is that of compassion. It is important that we come to realize that some problems are simply inevitable because we live in a fallen world. At some point in life all of us will experience the pain of some type of "bite." Therefore, my desire is to offer an in-depth look, and possibly a unique perspective, into the areas in which we can be bitten.

In a special time of prayer, God ministered a simple, yet powerful revelation to me: ***It's not the bite that destroys or kills, but the poison that comes with the bite***. There are many ways in which we can be bitten: the death of a loved one, a bad marriage, rejection, problems with our children, or even financial difficulties. Although some bites are inevitable, we can avoid poisons like bitterness, hatred, and unforgiveness which so often come along with the bite. How do we keep from being poisoned? One major way is by understanding the power and the authority God has given to us.

I pray that as you read this book God will minister deliverance and healing to your situation. May He grant you grace to maintain the right attitude, even when faced with great struggles. When all is said and done, you can say, "Although I was bitten, I refused to be poisoned."

                           In His Service,
                           Dr. Robbi Warren

Dedications

In memory of my mother and father (Lawrence and Dorothy Warren). You raised me to be the man that I am. Thank you for teaching me by example how to love and have compassion for others.

LaVelton and Trish, thanks for being there when I needed a family.

"Mother" Green, you are my spiritual mother. The love and support I've received from you and your family is priceless.

Mother Grayson and the Grayson family. Thanks for your prayers, support, and words of wisdom during many trying times.

I give thanks to God for my biological parents, William "Bubba" Warren (deceased) and Mary Francis Warren. Neither of you knew what God had in store for my life, but I am so grateful that you conceived me.

To my Pastor, Bishop James Tyson, and Christ Church family, thanks for being a true pastor and a strength. Your compassion and love for the ministry encourages me to continue in the faith.

Finally, this book is dedicated to all those who have been bitten by the devastation of life's experiences. May the God of glory give you insight and revelation to know that you don't have to be poisoned.

CHAPTER ONE

Paul Was Bitten, But Not Poisoned

Often, my prayer to God is similar to that of the disciples, "Lord teach me to pray." Now notice, they did not ask Jesus to teach them how to preach, work miracles, perform signs or wonders, but their passion was to have an intimate relationship with God through prayer. This should be the attitude of every believer in the church today. Only through prayer can we see the supernatural hand of God move in our lives. When believers embrace the privilege of sharing intimacy with the Lord, we will shift into a supernatural realm in which the works of Satan will literally be destroyed. I'm talking about prayer that is full of energy and is as intensified as the prayer that Jesus prayed in the Garden of Gethsemane (Luke 22:40-44). This was not just a mediocre prayer. Prayer still works!

Do You Know Your Position

Do you realize that we have the power to change things? *"The earnest [heartfelt, continued] prayer of a righteous man makes tremendous power available [dynamic in its working]"* (James 5:16, AMP). The Apostle Paul experienced this tremendous power and literally saw it at work in his life, and the lives of those around him. Although Paul warned the ship's crew that their lives would be in danger if they sailed; they disobeyed and sailed anyway. Even though Paul was affected (bit) by their decision, he did not allow it to affect his willingness to pray and seek God. In other words, he did not become poisoned. Paul prayed and God gave him an answer. *"For there stood by me this night the angel of God, whose I am, and whom I serve, saying, Fear not, Paul; thou must be brought before Caesar: and, lo, God hath given thee all them that sail with thee"* (Acts 27:23–24). Paul told the crew that even though the ship may begin to break up, no lives would be lost if only they would abide in the ship. You know the rest of the story—they all survived the storm. Paul's prayer made tremendous power available and the ship's crew was saved.

There is a powerful revelation here that we must grasp. After we have prayed, there must be a willingness on our part to remain in certain positions so that the glory of God will be revealed. We must develop the attitude, "No matter what happens; I will stay where God has placed me because I want to see His glory revealed in my life." Unfortunately, this is not the attitude of many believers today. Instead of allowing God to influence them, they are influenced by the flesh and are led by their carnal nature. Sometimes it's easier to base our actions on what is seen, heard, or felt, but if we're going to see the dynamic power of God working in our lives we've got to take a leap of faith. Now some may ask, "What do you mean?" We must trust God in spite of the way things seem.

Now let us examine why Paul's prayer was so effective. His life of obedience caused him to seek God even though he was in the midst of a storm, which was the safest place he could be. The pavilion of safety is *seeking* and *trusting* God, not necessarily the storms that we go through. When we consider that we have been bought with the priceless blood of Jesus, it should be an honor to walk by faith and not by sight knowing that we belong to Him. In this end time, the church must learn to align itself with the will of the Lord. We should not allow the storms of life to cause us to fret or fear. If all that God desires to accomplish in the earth through us is going to be completed, "*self*" has to die.

Reality Check

Sometimes salvation is presented to new converts as an easy out to life's problems. "Just give your life to Jesus," some say "and you will never face another battle again." This sounds like a good sales pitch, but this is far from the truth. It is an unbalanced representation of the true life of a believer. Words of influence such as these have caused many Christians to be stunted in their spiritual growth, and as a result, they give up when placed under pressure. We must realize that our spiritual muscles need exercise. There are many parts of our spiritual man that need to be developed. Here are a few: peace, temperance, love, strength, and faith. We must realize that all of these exist within us, but there is always room for growth, especially when God is developing our inward man to the full stature of Christ. Trials make a good workout! Take a look at what the Word of God says:

> *For everyone who continues to feed on milk is obviously inexperienced and unskilled in the doctrine of righteousness [of conformity to the divine will in purpose, thought, and action], for he is a mere infant [not able to talk yet]! But solid food is for full-grown men, for those whose senses and mental faculties are trained by practice to discriminate and distinguish between what is morally good and noble and what is evil and contrary either to divine or human law.*
> —Hebrews 5:13–14, AMP.

> *Yea, and all that will live godly in Christ Jesus shall suffer persecution.*
> —II Timothy 3:12

> *Nay, in all these things we are more than conquerors through him that loved us.*
> —Romans 8:37

As children of God we're going to go through trials and tribulations, *"These things I have spoken unto you, that in me ye might have peace, in the world ye shall have tribulation: but be of good cheer; I have overcome the world"* (John 16:33). Jesus overcame the world: *"greater is He that is in you than he that is in the world"* (I John 4:4). The good news is that we too have the power to overcome the world. Yes, the devil is allowed to test us at times so that we will learn how to place our total confidence in God, and not in ourselves. God desires to prove Himself to us, yet, at the same time He delights when we prove ourselves to Him. God also wants us to know from personal experience that He is Omnipotent (all powerful), Omniscient, (knows everything), and Omnipresent (present in all places at the same time). He is the true God.

As we exercise our spiritual muscles, lifting weights of tests and trials, we should never forsake the altar of prayer, for it is on the altar where we gain strength for the battle. Prayer is refreshing to the soul and will keep us from being spiritually dehydrated. Take another look at what the Word says:

> *For I reckon that the sufferings of this present time are not worthy to be compared with the glory which shall be revealed in us.*
> —Romans 8:18

The experiences that we encounter can in no way compare to the glory that will be revealed in us after we go through certain situations. Now consider heaven. What is going to make heaven so unique is knowing that all the trauma, tragedies, and horrible situations that we go through on earth will not exist there. Hallelujah!

Make the commitment to develop a steadfast mind when facing life's challenges. The reality is this: **we are in spiritual warfare**. It's time to become focused and sober minded. Demonic forces are bombarding many around the world; these forces influence weak Christians by creating confusion and disharmony within the Body of Christ and they immobilize others causing them to tolerate things that shouldn't be tolerated. Satan is very aware of who you are in Christ, but do you know who you are? This is why he uses his weapons of warfare to hinder your spiritual growth. The Spirit of God is saying, "Wake up, get on the firing line, you may not realize it, but you are armed and dangerous." "Pick up your weapons mighty men and women of God and run to the battle." The enemy doesn't care how much we sing, or preach, but he does not want the church to walk in the authority and anointing that God has given to us, because when we do, the works of the devil will be destroyed in our lives.

It takes boldness, humility, and spending quality time with God in order to maintain the level of anointing that is needed to destroy the works of the devil. When we are saturated with the presence of God, His character becomes so much a part of our lives that our very being affects the atmosphere around us, *"If my people, who are called by my name, shall humble themselves and pray and seek my face and turn from their wicked ways, then will I hear from heaven and will forgive their sin and will heal their land"* (II Chron. 7:14). God is looking for someone who will say, *"Lord, I surrender all."*

God is doing a new thing within the body of Christ. He's *shaking* everything that is not rooted and grounded in His Word. The only way that we are going to conquer this battle is to go back to old-time prayer, fasting, and believing the Word. The church of the living God is triumphant, bold, and strong in this end time. Are we going to be cowards and walk in fear, or are we going to believe God and walk in boldness?

SHAKE IT OFF

And when they were escaped, then they knew that the island was called Melita. And the barbarous people shewed us no little kindness: for *they kindled a **fire**, and received us every one, because of the present rain, and because of the cold. And when Paul had gathered a bundle of sticks, and laid them on the fire, there came a viper out of the heat, and fastened on his hand. And when the barbarians saw the venomous beast hang on his hand, they said among themselves, No doubt this man is a murderer, whom, though he hath escaped the sea, yet vengeance suffereth not to live. And he **shook off** the beast into the fire, and felt no harm.*

—Act 28:1–5

A lot can be learned from studying the life of the Apostle Paul. If ever there was a person who trusted God, the Apostle Paul definitely qualified. It took being thrown from his jackass and supernaturally blinded before he received the revelation of who Jesus was. Paul did not witness first hand the accounts of Jesus as the twelve Apostles did, but God's anointing was on his life for Apostleship and he received many revelations directly from the Lord through supernatural visitations. Paul's mission required that he dismantle some of the familiar teaching of the age to bring a balance between the letter of the Word (the law) and the Spirit. This caused irritation with many of his brethern.

Sometimes our commitment to walk in obedience to the Lord may cause our friends to reject us, for the scripture says, "*. . . I was wounded in the house of my friends*" (Zech. 13:6). Always remember that *obedience is better than sacrifice.*

Through many struggles Paul developed a genuine love for God and His people. "*For I could wish that myself were accursed from Christ for my brethren, my kinsmen according to the flesh*" (Rom. 9:3). The challenges he faced produced a passion in him to know Christ in an intimate way, "*That I may know him, and the power of his resurrection, and the fellowship of his sufferings, being made conformable unto his death*" (Phil. 3:10).

Paul had gotten to the point where he would not allow people to intimidate him. Not being intimidated is a major key to deliverance. So many believers in the church today are being intimidated by the devil, by people, and by situations. *"God hath not given us the spirit of fear; but of power, and of love, and of a sound mind"* (II Tim. 1: 7). There are too many insecure believers. Many have the revelation of who Jesus is, but have no revelation of who they are in Christ. Know that in spite of life's obstacles God has chosen you for the kingdom for such a time as this. God is on your side!

When Paul began to put the sticks on the fire, out of the heat came a viper. Notice, the viper did not come out of the fire, but the viper was *driven* out by the heat. Anytime we stir up the fire of God and cause the heat of the Spirit to generate to others, we can expect snakes (demons) to start moving about and come from every direction to try to damn what God has preordained us to do. Can you imagine the shock and terror of beholding such a sight that seemed to come from out of nowhere? Sounds like many of the devastating things we encounter day to day—divorce, disease, heartache, and the list goes on.

This *venomous beast* locked itself onto Paul's hand and hung there such a long time that the people who were looking became confused thinking that Paul was a murderer and was being punished for his actions. When you are in the midst of a battle, don't expect everyone to understand, or correctly perceive the spiritual war you're facing. Often times, as in this instance, the blame may be pointed toward you instead of Satan.

There are those who are just not spiritually minded. You can waste your time trying to explain your situation to them and they simply won't believe you, or have enough insight to see and perceive what you're going through. Your credibility as a Christian will be tested. **Keep your focus!** Paul shook the viper off into the fire of God. Some of you have been shaking "things" off, but God wants you to shake things off in Him, for He is a consuming fire (Heb. 12:29). When you simply shake "things" off, they may reattach to you and bite you again, sucking the life out of you. But when you shake it off in God, He will totally annihilate it.

Don't allow the devil to play games with your mind. Stand firm and let the devil know that *you* know that your Bible says, *"No weapon that is formed against you shall prosper, and every tongue that shall rise against you in judgment you shall show to be in the wrong . . ."* (Isa. 54:17, AMP.).

Because the barbarians perceived Paul to be a mere man, they were looking for him to swell up and fall dead suddenly. They were astonished when they saw no harm come to him. Medically, the only thing that actually cures a person from a venomous bite is an antidote. Poison literally will travel from the place of incision, into the blood stream, cause respiratory failure, and ultimately death. And the same applies to our spiritual being. *It's not the bite that kills you, it is the poison.*

The people did not realize that Paul had an antidote, a supernatural power at work in his system, a different blood flowing through his spiritual veins—the precious blood of Jesus. God did not allow Paul to be poisoned and killed because He anointed and appointed him to fulfill His purpose. He was predestined to be used by God.

Many people talk about destiny, but one definition of destiny is destination. And the way that you find your destination is by being sensitive to the leading of the Spirit of God. Destiny is not only natural—it is supernatural, it's the place God has designed for you. God has chosen you for destiny. When you have this revelation, then you will know that you have been uniquely made and chosen to fulfill God's purpose and plan. As we reflect on the descendants of Abraham, we see God's plan being executed when He said to Abram, *"Know of a surety that thy seed shall be a stranger in a land that is not theirs, and shall serve them; and they shall afflict them four hundred years; And also that nation, whom they shall serve, will I judge: and afterward shall they come out with great substance"* (Gen. 15:13–14). It's not about how we go through. It's about how we come out. That's why the Bible says in Romans 8:28, *"And we know that all things work together for good to them that love God, to them who are the called according to his purpose."* God has called us for His purpose, not our own. If more believers would understand and accept this truth, our lives would have less stress. We must understand that it is not our duty or job to make things work for our good, but it is our obligation, no matter what, to love God inspite of every situation that may occur in our lives. Then we will see that the outcome will be better than the outlook.

You may have been bitten and have the scars to prove it, but don't let the venom seep into your system and paralyze the works of God in your life. Remember that the devil can't penetrate the force field of the blood of Jesus. If he could he would have defeated Jesus, *but Jesus whipped him to an open shame*. When Satan sees the blood, he must pass over you. Stand in the liberty that Jesus has provided for you through His blood.

Most of us can probably think of something that has happened in our lives that was very devastating and should have taken us out. Some of us should not be alive today! But the goodness of the Lord has kept us and brought us to this point. When the enemy came in like a flood, the Spirit of the Lord lifted up a standard against him. If God were not on our side, we wouldn't have survived.

We may not know it, but there are people who are looking at us, just to see how we handle trials. When we gain the victory, in the spirit realm, the badge of honor glistens as a testimony for others to behold. It's a landmark that says, "Yes, you too can make it." The Bible says that we overcome by the blood of the

Lamb and the word of our testimony (Rev. 12:11). This is why it is important to proclaim the goodness and delivering power of God through our testimony, and not to complain about what we're going through. Always allow your mouth to speak forth praises. No matter what the devil throws at you, for in the end you will be victorious. If ever you find yourself in doubt or discouraged, take a look at what you've *been* through and how God delivered you. If He did it once, He'll do it again!

I've been in testimony services where I have felt like getting up and running out of the back door. Just hearing the defeating testimonies that come from believers saddens my heart. For instance, "Praise the Lord saints, I just don't think I can make it, you know the devil's busy." We should never give the devil any glory and honor. Sometimes as believers I think that we speak of the devil too often in our testimonies. God has given us the authority to speak to our mountains (test and trials), and tell them to move out of our way. It is never the will of God for us to speak in the negative. All of us will encounter battles in life, and we must realize that these are only temporary inconveniences, but they will cause development of character and integrity in us. In every mountain experience there is always a glory to be revealed. Think about it. Moses experienced the supernatural presence of God on the mountain and his face shone as God. Abraham, the father of faith, was tested and proven by God on a mountain, and even Jesus finished his mission on Mount Calvary.

Know this, we need the supernatural *strength* of the Lord to make it through any test because the joy of the Lord is our strength. Did you know that Satan has assigned demons to try to steal our joy? Don't accept the imps of gloom when they come your way. The enemy knows that all he has to do is weigh us down in some way by pushing the right button and we probably will loose our joy.

There is a potential danger that lies in the mouth of every

believer; its poison is fatal if released. The little member we call "the tongue" can unleash a world of unharnessed defeat, or build a universe of victories for the true conqueror. The Word of God is alive and very potent, but it can only become active in our situation when we put it in our mouths and proclaim what the Lord saith regarding our situation. Many say they're going to take back what the devil has stolen from them. But, there are some things the devil has not stolen; they were given to him. In some cases, we give the devil exactly what he wants by agreeing with his message of defeat. We give him our prayer life by becoming so busy with our daily affairs that we neglect spending valuable time with the Lord. We give him our children by confessing damaging words over their character. We give him our churches by not preaching and teaching the truth, for fear of losing members. What have you given the devil?

Recently, I shared with a precious saint that we must learn how to believe and trust God more. We need both trust and belief. After all the scripture declares that *"even the devils also believe, and tremble"* (James 2:19). They believe God, but do they trust God? To *trust* God means that a proven relationship of faith has been established between you and Him. You know beyond a shadow of a doubt that He won't let you down, even when situations don't quite turn out the way you expect them to.

One of the biggest dilemmas I see in this end time is a lack of trust. People are trying to make things happen rather than giving situations to the Lord and trusting him to handle them. Here's an example: often we try to *make* people get saved instead of trusting God to save them. The Holy Ghost equips us to be witnesses, not saviors. You have more influence than you can ever imagine. Your mere presence alone can have influence. A Holy Ghost-filled wife may encounter problems winning her unsaved husband to the Lord by bashing or nagging him about his ungodly behavior, rather she should allow her chaste conversation and holy lifestyle to influence him. Even if he doesn't obey the Word of God, she has the power to win him to the Lord through *her* obedience to the Word and her love (I Pet. 3:1). Our job is to live a life of influence. We must trust God to provide salvation. He does the *saving*. Our trust is built on Acts 2:39, *"The promise is unto you, and to your children, and to all that are afar off, even as many as the* **Lord** *our God shall call."*

Where to Place Your Focus

The Bible says that we are to seek first the kingdom of God and His righteousness and all these *things* shall be added unto us.

> *But seek, aim at and strive after first of all His kingdom and His righteousness (His way of doing and being right), and then all these things taken together will be given you besides.*
> —Matthew 6:33, AMP.

It would take a lifetime to truly seek the kingdom of God, but as we seek Him, He will add *things*. We must first exercise obedience to His Word. It is only when we seek Him that we gain the revelation of who He is and who we are in Him. In this passage, *kingdom* literally means the *sovereign realm* of God, the King's domain. God is sovereign in all dimensions. His authority is proven in every area of space: in heaven, in earth and under the earth, in your mind, your soul, your body, and your spirit. He knows what you are in need of before you ask. When we understand the sovereign rule of God and know that He sees into every area of our lives, then we will no longer seek to find the solution to our problem, but seek to find Him in the midst of our problem. His love and provision go so far beyond the moment of our temporal struggle. He's at the beginning, middle, and end of our situation all at the same time. The Lord is sovereign and He says, "Seek or desire My kingdom and My righteousness (the character of God), first, before you desire anything, even before you desire the solution to your problem. The solution will be *added unto you.*" God says, "Seek me daily and I will give you more of what you need and desire; the more you seek me, the more I'm going to bless you."

We must also seek His righteousness. How do we seek God's righteousness, or His character? Through prayer and consecration. But many are not seeking God to the magnitude that they should. This is mainly because they have been poisoned by the cares of this life (the world means more to them than God). Some have poisoned themselves by being controlled by the flesh and not by the Spirit. Maybe they haven't committed total spiritual suicide, but they have poisoned their systems with superficial junk. That is to say, only what you do for Christ will last and be counted in the end. We need our hearts and spirits cleansed.

It is amazing how many people appear to be spiritual a few "anxious" hours before midnight on New Year's Eve just because they think the Lord is about to come. ". . . *Oh, Lord! . . . You could come, I'm not ready, Jesus forgive me. Jesus*!" They hear a convicting message, go to the altar, repent, speak in tongues, and get baptized, but never gain a solid foundation, or commit to grow in the knowledge and wisdom of God. After a few days into the new year people go back to their same old ways, doing the same old things. Becoming a mature, strong Christian requires submission, diligence, and absolute surrender. God wants us to build a strong, lasting relationship with Him. We must not allow ourselves to become people who are looking for entertainment, and we as preachers must not allow ourselves to be entertainers. As men and women of God we must search for a deeper purpose. God is opening doors for the gospel to be heard like never before by way of mass media. I have never seen a day like this where the church has gained so much exposure. Yet, we must strive to seek

God even more.

This is why Paul was so powerful and so authoritative when it came to spiritual matters. He had a relationship with God. *"I count all things but loss for the excellency of the knowledge of Christ Jesus my Lord: for whom I have suffered the loss of all things, and do count them but dung, that I may win Christ"* (Phil. 3:8). In other words, I'm pursuing Christ. I'm going after him like a crazy man. I'm forgetting those things which are behind me and I'm reaching . . . I'm pressing toward the ultimate reward—a higher calling in Christ Jesus. It's not that he was trying to be deep. There's a difference between being "deep" and being "spiritual." There are a lot of "deep" people in the church, but not enough spiritual people. You see, those who are spiritual know how to bridle their tongue. Spiritual people will pray when no one else is praying. Spiritual people will fast even if their pastor doesn't call a fast. Spiritual people will lift their hands and praise God in the middle of difficult situations saying, "Lord you are my Jehovah Jireh, my provider." They will work when there appears to be no reward or acknowledgment in sight.

The only way to develop a spiritual mentality is to rid ourselves of things that clog us up. There are so many things that we must get rid of. There are some people and some past negative experiences that we have to get out of our system. Someone may say, "Well, this person really hurt me, and God should have stopped it before it happened." Sometimes God will allow certain situations to occur in our lives to get our attention. He removes our props so that we no longer lean on people, but we learn to lean on Him. God's desire is for His people to put their total trust in Him, but many of us have to fall before we remember that He alone is our strength.

CHAPTER TWO

Bit by Religion

Religion is simply man's search for God. My parents were very devout to their religious faith and served in the church faithfully. Dad was an honorable head deacon and Mom was an awesome church musician. I credit my love for music to my upbringing. I learned a lot from my parents about commitment and love for God. But, at the age of fifteen I began my personal journey searching for God. It all started after the death of a very close friend who was a star high school athlete. This made me realize that life is short even when you're young.

I was fortunate enough to have close friends in the neighborhood. Many of them were like brothers and sisters to me. One day my friend Johnny told me about something that happened to him in church. He had been baptized in the Holy Ghost. He said, "Robbi, you have to experience this." As a teenager this confused me greatly because I knew that my lifestyle of church going and dedication far exceeded his mischievous behavior. How could he have a spiritual experience that I didn't have? I didn't understand, but I knew that something different had happened to him. After telling my Mom what he said, her advice to me was, *"Well, son all I can tell you is to pray,"* so that's what I did. I said, *"Lord if this experience is real, give it to me."* God did just that. While visiting Johnny's church, I raised my hands to God during the altar call with simple childlike faith and a repentant heart, and God baptized me in the Holy Ghost. This experience came from God Almighty. After experiencing such a move of God in my life, I desired for everyone to have what I felt. It was out of this world!

Unfortunately, my parents were void of understanding and their *religious* background caused them not to be receptive to the Pentecostal experience. They discredited my godly encounter and said that it was one of fanaticism and that my brothers and I had been brainwashed. If that wasn't enough, on one Easter Sunday morning while attending the church where my brothers and I were raised, my father stood up in defiance of our experience and wanted us to deny the Baptism of the Holy Ghost and rejoin our old church. The Spirit of God said to me, "Don't move." My parents didn't understand that this was not a religious experience, but a God experience. It had nothing to do with joining a church or religion, but it was because the fire God gave to us was so real that we couldn't deny it. The result for us was a *harsh* beating and strict instructions never to go back to *that* church again. Even as a child I knew that I had found God in a way that I didn't have Him before. Pure religion should always usher you into a life-changing experience that provokes you into a worshiping relationship with God. I had experienced the power of God through religion, but at the same time I had been *bitten* and was experiencing the *poison* of not being able to enjoy the liberty of the presence of God.

Webster's New World Dictionary defines religion as *"the belief in and worship of God or gods, a specific system of belief, worship, often involving a code of ethics."* There are so many different kinds of religions in the world—Christianity, Buddhism, Hinduism, Islam—when a person becomes hungry for God it's easy to get caught in the web of choice. Satan knows this and he uses the deception of vain religious experiences to pacify the hungry heart and blind many from the truth of the Gospel of Jesus Christ. Unfortunately, many religions embrace idol worship. This is evident in cultic religions. The result of a person joining these types of religion is bondage. A soul becomes bound to the evil spirits that accompany such doctrines. In many cases the person becomes demonically possessed. Just because a person says that they're part of a religion does not mean that they are serving or worshipping THE Creator. Remember the scripture says:

> *Wherefore lay apart all filthiness and superfluity of naughtiness, and receive with meekness the engrafted word, which is able to save your souls. But be ye doers of the word, and not hearers only, deceiving your own selves. For if any be a hearer of the word, and not a doer, he is like unto a man beholding his natural face in a glass: For he beholdeth himself, and goeth his way, and straightway forgetteth what manner of man he was. But whoso looketh into the perfect law of liberty, and continueth therein, he being not a forgetful hearer, but a doer of the work, this man shall be blessed in his deed. If any man among you seem to be religious, and bridleth not his tongue, but deceiveth his own heart, this man's religion is vain. Pure religion and undefiled before God and the Father is this, To visit the fatherless and widows in their affliction, and to keep himself **unspotted from the world.***
> —James 1:21–27

If there is a "pure" and undefiled religion, then there is an "impure" and defiled religion. Any religion that does not embrace the Gospel of Jesus Christ is defiled. The only way to become *unspotted from the world* is to believe on Him that overcame the world, and that is Jesus Christ, the life giver. *"In Him was life and the life was the light of men"* (John 1:4). Not only is there life in Jesus, but there is truth because He is the Truth.

When people are searching for God they are searching for the power that will change their lives forever. During my travels, I've encountered many religions that condone traditions and doctrines that are not biblically sound. With our many differences in Christianity we must not embrace the attitude of just seeking a religion, for often times that's what causes many of us to have views that are not necessarily biblical. For instance, when we speak of Pentecostalism, we must realize that we are really speaking of an experience that happened during the time of the feast of Pentecost. Jesus proclaimed to His disciples that He would send another Comforter and during Pentecost, the outpouring of the Holy Ghost took place. Many associate this experience with denominationalism—which is a false perception. It is amazing to me how we fight over titles that supposedly validate our various religions. Jesus never intended for it to be this way. For He said, *"Upon this rock I will build my church and the gates of hell shall not prevail against it."* Now understand what the scripture says. It doesn't say I will build denominations or titles. We that are a part of the church that Jesus has built must understand that we have been given power over all the powers of the enemy. Therefore, it is our legal right to utilize this power because of the authority God has given us.

When we don't understand certain truths such as these and point people toward doctrine more than the Gospel of Jesus Christ, we've missed the call of the great commission and rob people of the life-changing experience of knowing who Jesus really is. The Pharisees and Sadducees had this problem. "No, Jesus," they said, "you can't heal on the Sabbath, it's against the *law.*" In other words, it was against the normal way that they were use to doing things. We must be careful that we do not focus so much on the letter of the Word that we miss the Spirit behind the Word.

> *And it came to pass, that he went through the corn fields on the Sabbath day; and his disciples began, as they went, to pluck the ears of corn. And the Pharisees said unto him, Behold, why do they on the Sabbath day that which is not lawful? And he said unto them, Have ye never read what David did, when he had need, and was an hungred, he, and they that were with him? How he went into the house of God in the*

days of Abiathar the high priest, and did eat the shewbread, which is not lawful to eat but for the priests, and gave also to them which were with him? And he said unto them, The sabbath was made for man, and not man for the sabbath: Therefore the Son of man is Lord also of the sabbath. And he entered again into the synagogue; and there was a man there which had a withered hand. And they watched him, whether he would heal him on the sabbath day; that they might accuse him. And he saith unto the man which had the withered hand, Stand forth. And he saith unto them, Is it lawful to do good on the sabbath days, or to do evil? to save life, or to kill? But they held their peace. And when he had looked round about on them with anger, being grieved for the hardness of their hearts, he saith unto the man, Stretch forth thine hand. And he stretched it out: and his hand was restored whole as the other.
—Mark 2:23–28; Mark 3:1–5

The normal way of doing things is not always God's way. When we develop the mentality that we've got God figured out, then we are operating in error. This will always be a hindrance to any move of God. Jesus exposed the hearts of the Pharisees by asking them if they had a donkey that had fallen into a ditch on the sabbath would they rescue it. Of course, the response was yes. It's amazing that certain rules only apply when it's convenient, but can be broken by those in authority. There are also various doctrines and standards that many denominations embrace, but when certain situations arise among leadership, then these doctrines and standards don't apply. This is what is called being biased. When rules only apply to a certain sect and can be broken by those in authority when it's convenient, then the tradition and doctrine of man's religion has become a substitute for the power of God. Therefore, it will be difficult for the church to experience a consistent flow of the Spirit of God. This is why Jesus said, *"You nullify the word of God by your tradition that you have handed down"* (Mk 7:13, NIV).

There is a great danger when we don't allow the word of God to be effective: souls will not be saved. When there is a need, God will do whatever it takes to meet it, even if it's something out of the ordinary. In the above passage of scripture, King David had a need. He was hungry. Eating the shewbread was unheard of, but he did it without penalty. How many people come to church time and time again desiring to experience a move of God, but still leave hungry and empty. What makes the Word of God to no effect? *The tradition of men*. We must understand that Jesus is Lord even over our *standards of tradition.* When we don't allow him to be, we've placed ourselves in the stead of God. The Apostle Paul dealt with the traditions of men when he stood up for Gentiles that had given their lives to God who had not been circumcised. This was a big problem. Circumcision had been passed down from generation to generation. However, Paul unveiled the truth, which was that God was not concerned about the outward appearance, but rather the circumcision of the heart of man.

> *When Peter came to Antioch, I opposed him to his face, because he was clearly in the wrong. Before certain men came from James, he used to eat with the Gentiles. But when they arrived, he began to draw back and separate himself from the Gentiles because he was afraid of those who belonged to the circumcision group. The other Jews joined him in his hypocrisy, so that by their hypocrisy even Barnabas was led astray. When I saw that they were not acting in line with the truth of the gospel, I said to Peter in front of them all, "You are a Jew, yet you live like a Gentile and not like a Jew. How is it, then, that you force Gentiles to follow Jewish customs? "We who are Jews by birth and not 'Gentile sinners' know that a man is not justified by observing the law, but by faith in Jesus Christ. So we, too, have put our faith in Christ Jesus that we may be justified by faith in Christ and not by observing the law, because by observing the law no one will be justified. "If, while we*

seek to be justified in Christ, it becomes evident that we ourselves are sinners, does that mean that Christ promotes sin? Absolutely not! If I rebuild what I destroyed, I prove that I am a lawbreaker. For through the law I died to the law so that I might live for God. I have been crucified with Christ and I no longer live, but Christ lives in me. The life I live in the body, I live by faith in the Son of God, who loved me and gave himself for me. I do not set aside the grace of God, for if righteousness could be gained through the law, Christ died for nothing!
—Galatians 2:11–21, NIV

We must examine our hearts even when it comes to simple things, like water baptism for example. Do we worship the water? Are we more concerned about seeing a person get baptized and speak in tongues than we are at making sure they remain saved, become doers of the Word, and grow to a solid level of maturity in Christ. Are we more interested in increasing our church roll numbers than we are at making sure people have an understanding of living a life that is unspotted from the world? Have we been bitten by religion?

I was bitten by religion when God filled me with His Spirit. I found that even in the assembly that I was a member of there were many religious views that were not biblically sound. One of the views in that church was, "Legislation without Scriptural Validation." This means that a religious doctrine is instituted by man, but has little to do with scripture, spiritual character, or integrity. Unfortunately, I found that this particular church was very prejudiced. They were biased when it came to blacks and whites intermingling or being married to each other, but would allow Latin Americans to marry Caucasians. Yet, when it came to African-Americans, regardless of feelings or desires, it was not permitted. Because of religious views that were not biblically sound, a considerable division was caused among people in the congregation. In scripture, God struck Miriam with leprosy because of her prejudiced disposition toward Moses marrying Zipporah, a black woman. Many religious institutions teach their own personal convictions rather than teaching how to be sensitive to the Holy Ghost, which will cause one to understand the Word of God more effectively. There is nothing wrong with traditions or ideologies as long as they are biblically sound and reflect a balance between the letter of the Word and the Spirit of the Word. *"Who also hath made us able ministers of the New Testament; not of the letter, but of the spirit: for the letter killeth, but the spirit giveth life"* (II Cor. 3:6).

When beliefs cause bias or prejudice, in any religion, then we can clearly say that religion is not of God. When God looks at a man, He does not see black or white, or any other color for that matter. He looks at the heart. *"Then Peter opened his mouth, and said, Of a truth I perceive that God is no respecter of persons: But in every nation he that feareth him, and worketh righteousness, is accepted with him"* (Acts 10:34–35*).*

Many people have been bitten by man-made religions and the separations they create. Man has even created religions contrary to the relationships that God instituted for man to have with one another. This is very serious. Some religions are extremely segregated. Many people don't realize that the Ku Klux Klan profess to be a religious organization. We can see and feel the effects of the racial hatred of this group. One sect of Muslims base their religion on certain biblical principles, but hatred is found throughout their sect. We know that *God is love* to everyone, not just one particular group of people. God loves all mankind. All mankind is a part of God, regardless of race. We all are precious in His sight. The Word says that God is no respecter of persons. He has not ostracized anyone. Religion is man's search for God and searching for God has bitten many precious people because the enemy often takes advantage of their zealousness. We have searched for God in places that have part, but not all truth. We have searched for Him in all the wrong places.

The Bible clearly lets us know that we cannot love Him whom we have not seen and hate our brother that we see daily. If we cannot bridle our tongue, then our religion is in vain. This constitutes the attitude that we must have a spirit of humility, not to discount religion, but to understand what religion is.

People have been bitten by certain ideologies which they believe religion stands for. If what they believe is not compatible to what God has ordained, then that religion is vain. It is not the bite of religion that will kill us. It is the poison in the bite. The poison of religion can get into our system and cause us to do things like hate our brethren.

The Pharisees were a religious sect, but because of their religious views, they could not accept Jesus Christ, the Lord and Savior of the world. They had been bitten and poisoned. The Bible poses the question, "How can the blind lead the blind except they both fall into a ditch?" So we must understand that religion should lead us into a relationship with God, not a cult. We are not to become so controlled by a man or a woman that we cannot pray, fast, or seek God independently. Any time a religion takes complete control of our being, the will of God cannot be an active force in your life. God has called us all to be *free* moral agents. *Where the Spirit of the Lord is, there is liberty.*

Now after reading the various things that have been said concerning religion, we must note that we are not against any religion that glorifies and reverences Jesus Christ as Lord, Savior, and soon coming King. However, those who have been bitten and poisoned to the degree that humanity, animals, and images have become their focal point and worship, are in error. For the Bible declares unto us that there are some that would rather serve the creature more than the Creator. There are demonic spirits that have been released against mankind to cause him to rebel against the Word of God. We must understand that the purpose of our worship and service is only to God, even though God has instructed us to serve one another we must rightly divide the Word of God. There are those that are in leadership that have a tendency to take scriptures out of context. God never intended for anything to take His place when it comes to worship. For the Bible lets us know that the Lord our God is one Lord and it also warns us that we should have no other God before Him. Anytime leaders use their religion or religious views to exalt themselves by manipulating others, then witchcraft is present. We must not allow ourselves to be used by the enemy to deceive others, so therefore, we all must constantly stay before God for guidance.

CHAPTER THREE

Bit by Inferiority

Inferiority is one of the biggest problems many people face in our present society. "What do I mean by this statement?" Being inferior causes one to have feelings of lower rank as well as feelings of doubt and instability, and may cause one to be double minded when faced with important decisions. When a person is faced with inferiority, he or she thinks others have more value than they. I'm reminded of a particular story in the Word of God where an individual was traveling in a far country and he called his servants and gave them money to invest. Now this parable is fitting for us today. Notice what happened. He gave one five, another two, and the other one talent. This powerful story unfolds the character of a person who feels inferior.

> *For the kingdom of heaven is as a man traveling into a far country, who called his own servants, and delivered unto them his goods. And unto one he gave five talents, to another two, and to another one; to every man according to his several ability; and straightway took his journey. Then he that had received the five talents went and traded with the same, and made them other five talents. And likewise he that had received two, he also gained other two. But he that had received one went and digged in the earth, and hid his lord's money.*
>
> —Mathew 25:14–18

Know What You Possess

Talent in the above passage is actually money. But consider a talent to be any ability that you possess. The man who had only one talent chose to bury it instead of investing it to increase his resources. Why? He didn't realize that *the talent was truly valuable, but its value could only be manifested as he utilized it.* Instead of being proud of his one talent, he compared it to others. If you don't know what you possess, you will never be able to effectively use it for the kingdom of God. Your *talent* can be any ability or gift that God has entrusted you with, no matter how small it may seem. The servant who buried his talent had problems beyond inferiority. In fact, there are many layers that make up the house of inferiority. Here are a couple: fear and slothfulness.

I Was Afraid

The toughest layer to remove is fear. The servant's response to his lord was, "I was afraid." Notice, the lord gave each servant talents according to *their* ability. God never entrusts us with something we don't have the ability to cause to expand for his glory. If God says you have the ability, who are you to say you do not. Fear must be combated with faith, faith in God, yes; but, also faith in knowing that God trusts you with His investment. The servant hid his talent in the earth instead of scattering it throughout. There are many avenues that you can utilize to scatter your talent, but it will never be effective in the ground.

Slothfulness

The hand of the diligent shall bear rule: but the slothful shall be under tribute.
—Proverbs 12:24

The sad part is that the servant knew what to do. He just didn't do it. He chose to bury his talent rather than apply himself to fulfill the Lord's command. How many times have we chosen the easy way out? Slothfulness always has two followers: procrastination and excuses. The cultivating of any gift from God requires work, hard work. But the reward is much sweeter than the labor. Faithfulness over little will always bring you into a power of ruling over *the much* that you thought you could not conquer. The servants that sowed their talents were called *good* and *faithful* and were able to enter into the *joy of Lord*. Joy is an awesome and much needed thing in anything we do. Without contentment that comes from God even the smallest task becomes a burden.

> *Then he which had received the one talent came and said, Lord, I knew thee that thou art an hard man, reaping where thou hast not sown, and gathering where thou hast not strawed: And I was afraid, and went and hid thy talent in the earth: lo, there thou hast that is thine. His lord answered and said unto him, Thou wicked and slothful servant, thou knewest that I reap where I sowed not, and gather where I have not strawed: Thou oughtest therefore to have put my money to the exchangers, and then at my coming I should have received mine own with usury. Take therefore the talent from him, and give it unto him which hath ten talents. For unto every one that hath shall be given, and he shall have abundance: but from him that hath not shall be taken away even that which he hath. And cast ye the unprofitable servant into outer darkness: there shall be weeping and gnashing of teeth.*
> —Matthew 25:24–30

WHO'S MIRROR ARE YOU LOOKING THROUGH?

Sometimes the spirit of jealousy will show up when inferiority is present. If the devil can't smother your potential by causing you to bury your *talent*, he certainly will try to clog your spirit with jealousy against your brother or sister, especially when their life of faithfulness has caused them to walk in the level of blessing that you desire.

One reason people become jealous is they spend more time looking through the window of those who have reaped the benefits of being faithful with their gifts and abilities, rather than taking inventory of their own talents. Once you gain knowledge as to "who you are" rather than "who you're not," then there is no need to be jealous because *you will* understand that God has fashioned and designed *you* specifically for a task in life that only you can accomplish. Your focus should be geared toward displaying a spirit of excellence in all that *you* do and it won't be a problem to give glory to God for what He's doing in the lives of others.

The Bible says that we should measure ourselves by God's rule (II Cor. 10:12–13). In other words, we don't measure ourselves with other people. We shouldn't judge ourselves based on someone else's success. If you encounter an old high school classmate who's driving a top-of-the-line luxury car and you're still driving the same 15-year-old vehicle that's followed by *a cloud of smoke*, inferiority might kick in. If we feel like someone else is better looking than we are, then unfortunately, we experience feelings of inferiority to that person and may walk around feeling inadequate and worthless. But this is not how it should be.

Society seems to esteem those who are of a fair and flawless complexion. The media helps to perpetuate the myth that those who have a certain look such as straight or curly hair or a super model's physique are the types that society favors. We are to judge the interior, not the exterior. Even though we have been bitten by society's standards, we must realize that we, as people of God, must look at our fellow man in the same way that God does. No man knows the heart, but God Himself. The enemy tries to take advantage of us through psychological manipulation. It's a mind thing. What we see and hear, and how we perceive them will dictate our mentality. The devil uses inferiority complexes to cause division among people. As believers we have to rise above this way of thinking.

Moses was a fugitive and he had a speech impediment, these

were major inferiority complexes. He didn't think he could accomplish the mission God set before him. But God said, *"Go and I will be with your mouth and teach thee what thou shalt say."* Because of Moses' inferiority God sent Aaron with Moses to speak for him. God desires to manifest His supernatural power even in our infirmities. God's power was in Moses's mouth, not in Aaron's speech. It was only when Moses told Aaron what to say that Aaron's words were effective. Sometimes because of our complexes God is not able to reveal Himself in us to the magnitude that He desires. Moses was *bitten* by inferiority, but he did not allow himself to be *poisoned*. He became one of the greatest men of biblical times.

Jeremiah said, *"Lord, I can't speak, I'm just a child"* (Jer. 1:4–6). Because of his stature and his age, he felt that he was inferior, incapable of doing what the Lord requested of him. But God said, *"I formed thee, I knew thee even before you were in the belly . . . before you came out of your mother's womb."* The woman of Samaria in John 4 who went to the well was aware of the attitude that the Jews had toward Samaritans. She felt inferior and asked Jesus why He asked her to draw water for Him, being that He was a Jew and Jews had no dealings with Samaritans. She had such an inferiority complex that she felt she was unworthy to even draw water for Him. She felt like she was nothing.

GOD'S MIRROR

God sees you as an in intricate part of His plan. It is vital that you understand your place in the kingdom, for it's only when you understand your place that you can truly walk in that place. Clearly we have not been called according to our purpose, but to the purpose of God. This being so, we must understand that God has called us out of darkness into His marvelous light. Inferiority complexes are not of God. We are all God's children. We are all precious in His sight. If God has given us His Spirit and has drawn us out of darkness, we must realize that He has done it for His divine purpose. When you understand the purposes of God you will understand that you have been divinely set up to fill a call that's far beyond your thoughts and plans. You must know where you fit in the plan, so that you will be able to capitalize on your gifts and talents, rather than someone else's—use it or lose it.

> *For the body is not one member, but many. If the foot shall say, Because I am not the hand, I am not of the body; is it therefore not of the body? And if the ear shall say, Because I am not the eye, I am not of the body; is it therefore not of the body? If the whole body were an eye, where were the hearing? If the whole were hearing, where were the smelling? But now hath God set the members every one of them in the body, as it hath pleased him. And if they were all one member, where were the body? But now are they many members, yet but one body. And the eye cannot say unto the hand, I have no need of thee: nor again the head to the feet, I have no need of you. Nay, much more those members of the body, which seem to be more feeble, are necessary: And those members of the body, which we think to be less honourable, upon these we bestow more abundant honour; and our uncomely parts have more abundant comeliness. For our comely parts have no need: but God hath tempered the body together, having given more abundant honour to that part which lacked. That there should be no schism in the body; but that the members should have the same care one for another.*
>
> —I Corinthians 12:14–25

There are classes of people in our society who have made it their top priority to make people feel inferior. There are white supremacy groups, politicians, "famous" people, and individuals who derive pleasure in elevating themselves and abasing others. This can be seen from the days of slavery. Even today many blacks have inferiority complexes. They feel like they can't attain to better things in life. We see this trend even in the church. Though we say that we are spiritual, there are divisions and "cliques" in many of God's churches. This is a serious problem because people have been bitten, thinking they can't fit in. On their jobs, children of God are working without advancing because they have inferiority complexes. They're working hard and in some cases, they're doing all the work, causing the company's stock and productivity to increase, yet they continue to be burdened by feelings of inadequacy which hinder them from putting forth an effort to apply for promotions or salary increases. These feelings keep us from owning property and businesses, or having the proper financing that we feel we need to accomplish and fulfill our desires and dreams . The Apostle Paul said, *"I can do all things through Christ, which strengthen me."* Inferiority causes us to be negative, not just toward each other, but also within ourselves. It causes us to have an attitude of doubt. As a man *thinketh* in his heart so is he. Your perception of yourself will be projected into the world around you. It will determine how you are perceived and often will cause a cycle of events in your own personal life, especially mentally. God has made each of us unique in our own right. He has groomed us and there is not one who is superior over another.

You may not be a CEO who owns a major corporation. You may not be graced to be a pastor, bishop, apostle, or prophet. Perhaps you're not called to be a husband or wife at this time. However, know that the Bible says that the one who is least among us is greatest in the kingdom. The Bible even says that the one who is last shall be first and the one who is first shall be last. Jesus was King of Kings and Lord of Lords, but He was also the one who was born in a stable. He did not allow His situation or His circumstances to dictate His way of thinking no matter what anyone else thought about Him.

So even though you may have been bitten by an inferiority

complex, allow God to heal your mind and heal your spirit. Present your body, a living sacrifice, holy and acceptable unto God, who is your Lord, and *"be ye not conformed to this world but be ye transformed by the renewing of your mind"* (Rom. 12:2). Start thinking positive. There is no better time than now. Understand that God has called you for so much more. God has ordained you to be who you are. You have been so uniquely made, and no one can take that away from you. Why let the enemy allow you to feel inferior? Take what you have and use it to the best of your ability. Display a spirit of excellence in all that you do. Use your talents for God's glory. It is not God's intent for us to measure ourselves with others. Allow God to look at your heart and let Him decide for Himself.

CHAPTER FOUR

Bit by Failure

I want to begin this chapter by saying that failure is not fatal. I'm reminded of a basketball player who didn't make the varsity team in high school, but despite this "set back," he kept perfecting his talent and he became one of the greatest basketball players of all time. His name is Michael Jordan. Failure can bring about an attitude of success if you allow it to, an attitude that creates stronger work ethics and a stronger drive to excel.

We classify ourselves as failures when we try something and it doesn't reach the expectation that we anticipated. It is then that we label ourselves as failures. But even though we have been bitten by *failing* at a certain task it doesn't mean we should allow ourselves to become poisoned, labeling ourselves as *failures.* Remember it is not the bite that is fatal, it is the poison that comes from the bite.

One example of someone who felt like a failure was Peter when he denied Jesus. *"And the Lord said, Simon, Simon, behold, Satan hath desired to have you, that he may sift you as wheat: But I have prayed for thee, that thy faith fail not: and when thou art converted, strengthen thy brethren"* (Luke 22:31–32). Peter had good intentions. He said, *"Lord; I'm willing to go with you into prison, even unto death."* But then Jesus told him, *"Before the cock doth crow three times, thou shalt thrice deny me."* In verse 60, as the cock is crowing, Peter responded, *"I was not with him."* The Bible tells us that Jesus turned and gave him a look, which caused Peter to remember what the Lord had prophesied to him. We are told that Peter went out and wept bitterly because he felt that he had failed. But, Jesus knew what would happen even before it happened. Isn't it wonderful to know that God knows everything before it happens. The whole situation went according to God's plan—God wanted to reveal to Peter his frailty and what was truly in his heart. Sometimes it takes failing in order for God to reveal to us what's really in our heart. It's only when our heart is revealed that we can overcome the undercurrent secrets that it holds. Peter may have been bitten by failure, but in no wise was he poisoned by failure. In fact, the experience caused him to be stronger in his spiritual walk. Many of us feel that we have failed in many avenues of our lives. I've experienced this feeling before. After I was saved, I went through a major trial. I lost hope and became devastated due to life's battles, so I resorted to drugs. I took drugs for one week. As a result, I stopped preaching and quit the ministry. I felt that I had failed God, in fact, I knew that I had. But God reminded me of the things that He had put in me, the investments that He made in my life and His unconditional love for me. God is not a failure. When His investment is on the inside of us, we are not failures. As believers we must apply what Paul told the church at Phillippi, "Being confident of this very thing that He which hath begun a good work in you will perform it until the day of Jesus Christ." During this episode in my life I followed Paul's instructions and put my confidence in the Lord. Although I'd failed myself as well as God, I still trusted God more than I trusted my failure. And I found out that even though I had failed, I was not a failure and I began to allow the Spirit to lead me into destiny.

LIVE AND LEARN

We may feel that we've failed in our marriages, in raising our children, and in many other areas. Our lives may seem to crumble before our very eyes, but this does not mean that we are failures. Sometimes *failure* can be God's way of getting our attention. He allows situations and circumstances to take place in our lives for our betterment. Now, sometimes failure can be a product of sin. If sin is the culprit, then we must deal with it. The best way is through true repentance. Repentance is the first step in allowing the will of God to take precedence in our lives. It is important that we have God-fearing Christians in our lives that help us to understand and submit to the will of God.

Sometimes it takes setbacks in order for God to get our attention. For instance, we may lose a job because God has a better job for us. We may have a failed relationship because God has a better relationship for us. The key is treating each experience as a learning experience. We can learn what our strengths and weaknesses are. In similar experiences we can learn what to do and what not to do, what works and what doesn't work, what wins and what loses. Don't be afraid to evaluate the situation for future reference. "... *And we know that all things work together for good to them that love God, to them who are the called according to his purpose*" (Rom. 8:28).

This is the attitude that we should have as we go through life. The Lord will never allow us to lose something without giving us something better. The prophet Elijah sat under a juniper tree depressed because Jezebel threatened to kill him. In desperation he wanted to give up and just quit. He felt *like* a failure. But, God told Elijah, "I have seven thousand that have not bowed to Baal." In other words, God was telling Elijah that he had other brothers and sisters that were standing with him in spite of the threats from Jezebel. Therefore, don't allow yourself to feel that you are a failure. Get back into position, for God will fulfill His purpose in your life and use you according to His plan.

Build a Fortified City
The Bible says that we are the light of the world, but what's the use in having light if there's no place to store it so that it will shine

and radiate for God's glory? Our lights shine as a *"city set on a hill that cannot be hidden"* (Matt. 5:14). Before you can gleam you must have a city to gleam in. You must build your city. When failure is experienced, unfortunately, many hopes and dreams come to ruin and the gates of your city may not even be recognizable. It takes time, prayer, and a lot of hard work to build a city, but beyond that, it takes a fresh outlook on life. The Holy Ghost can give you the fresh wind you need to renew your mind and energize your spirit. Just one building alone must have the proper foundation so that it can support a strong structure and this is only a minor part to building a city. You still have to pave roads, erect beautification, and add traffic signals.

"Fear of failure" is the wrong equipment to keep in your spiritual toolbox. Your hopes and dreams must always be built on the solid foundation of Jesus Christ the Lord and there is no fear in HIM. Know that God's love is perfect, and perfect love casts out fear. His expectation for you is not failure, neither is His love predicated on whether you succeed or fail. HIS love is unconditional. Wrap that around your heart as you move forward. As you build and fortify yourself by placing HIS Word deep within your heart, know that you are an overcomer. Allow the places where you have failed to be healed and begin to build your confidence again in HIM. As you're bulldozing the ruin of past failures, take counsel from the Holy Ghost as to how, when, and where to build again. Don't be people conscious. Remember the past is the past.

Forget Where You've Been to Get Where You're Going

When we are on the battlefield of life, we are there to win the war. God allows things to happen in our lives for his divine purpose. We may be bitten, but we don't have to be poisoned. Paul said, *"Brethren, I count not myself to have apprehended: but this one thing I do, forgetting those things which are behind, and reaching forth unto those things which are before, I press toward the mark for the prize of the high calling of God in Christ Jesus"* (Phil. 3:13–14). Paul said he was going to forget the good things as well as the bad things. This is what we must do when we fail. We must press on, not look back to where we have been or where we have failed, but look forward to where God is taking us. Where we have been in the past, and where we have failed in the past can prepare us for where we are going in the future. Don't allow the bite to poison you. Don't lie down and die. You are not a failure. You can do all things through Christ which strengthens you.

One of the most powerful things to behold is a child when he takes his first step. After many falls, stumbles, and plunders he gains enough confidence to go for it again. Soon falling isn't a big "to do" anymore, in fact the toddler expects to walk in spite of the falls. Can you imagine that after falling and sometimes very hard, the toddler's instinct causes him to continue to try and walk? Even as a baby his determination is unbelievable. This must be a God-given gift that's given to all of us when we fall and fail. Notice, the first time he may whimper a little, but then he gets up, secures his feet, and goes for it again. It takes the guidance of a parent to watch him, coach him, and love him through his learning process. Years of practice enable him to walk like a man. Your heavenly Father is there to coach you through your learning process. But, in order for your legs to gain strength you must exercise your faith, otherwise your muscles will be too weak to walk. Walk like the man or woman God has created you to be. You are not a failure.

For a just man falleth seven times, and riseth up again.
—Proverbs 24:16

CHAPTER FIVE

Bit by Success

At some point in life we all desire to be successful. Sometimes, I feel that our definition of success as believers has been clouded by the system of the world and its standard. For example, owning a certain type of home, car or even having a prestigious job. Now don't be confused, having these things in life is certainly a blessing, but we must realize that things such as these don't make the person. It's important to realize that the world we live in is not perfect because of Adam and Eve's fall in the garden. For this reason many gloat in what they call success. Unfortunately when they cross the line of success they begin to look down upon others. God never meant for success to be based upon the material things a person has, but it should be determined by one's character, attitude, and willingness to share and give to others. God spoke to Joshua, giving him specific instructions as to how to gain *good* success and this came through Joshua's obedience and meditation in the Word of God (Josh. 1:8). We can acquire good success if we maintain the right spirit when we're blessed, but the Word of God must be the balancer! If there is no balance, then being poisoned is inevitable.

Successful Giants of the Past

The Lord *has pleasure in the prosperity of his servants* (Ps. 35:27). Abraham, the Father of Faith, had wealth and possessions. Even Job was a very wealthy man. But, these men did not place their confidence in their material possessions. When Job faced the most devastating time in his life, he tore his garment, fell to the ground, and worshipped saying, *"Naked came I out of my mother's womb, and naked shall I return thither: the LORD gave, and the Lord hath taken away, blessed be the name of the LORD"* (Job 1:21). His material possessions did not override his relationship with God, because he did not sin verbally against God. Even during the time of great turmoil in his life, he maintained his integrity and God gave him double for his trouble. Abraham's willingness to sacrifice his son of promise—Isaac—proved his obedience and faith toward God, not in what he possessed. The prophet Elisha's success was not in material things, but in the double portion anointing that he received from God Almighty. He walked in that double portion anointing and saw twice as many miracles as his mentor Elijah. All of these men's success was based on their relationship with the Lord, *not* in the blessings that the Lord provided—whether the blessing was spiritual or natural.

Unsuccessful Shadows of the Past

There were others in scripture who acquired success, but were *poisoned* by it. As Saul moved into the position of king (a high level of success), he became vain and as a result began to do things contrary to God's instruction—which caused God to strip him of his kingship. Later Saul turned toward sorcery and consulted the dead. He worshipped his position more than the one who put him in position.

The fight for power and prestige can cause the best of friends to be at odds. Success can destroy people quicker than failure. Judas had this problem. This was a man who was discipled and befriended by the King of Glory, but he loved money more than he loved God. He betrayed his Lord and Savior for thirty pieces of silver. What about those who profess to be preachers, pastors or evangelists that minister for the sake of money yet have no concern for the soul? They enjoy the glory of a lavish lifestyle, fame and

The Venom

When we *think* that we are successful, we must be extremely careful, for the Bible cautions us that *if a man thinketh that he stand, take heed lest he fall.* Many of us feel that having houses, money and cars make us successful individuals. There are many people who are successful by society's standards, but they have no compassion for others, no peace, no joy and no hope. This is why many whom society has labeled as successful end up throwing it all away by an act of suicide. Material possessions will never bring fulfillment. I believe the ultimate success that one can achieve is being totally sold out to God and making it to heaven. The Bible says that God wants us to prosper and be in good health even as our soul prospers. The reference of the soul in this passage of scripture is so frequently overlooked, particular when many teachings focus on prosperity being simply that of material gain, rather than the whole man, spirit, soul and body.

The story of the rich man and Lazarus teaches us a good lesson. The rich man had it all. Lazarus only wanted the crumbs that fell from the rich man's table. No matter what the rich man had nor what Lazarus didn't have, they both came to the place of death. Lazarus ended up in the bosom of Abraham, and the rich man lifted up his eyes in torment. Some may say that God was unfair, but we have to look at the message conveyed. Jesus stated in one passage of scripture that when you've "done it" to the least of these, you've done it unto me. It wasn't so much what the rich man did, but what he didn't do. He didn't show an attitude of compassion or concern. He became drunk on his own success, which caused him to neglect his brother. Notice, what the Word of God conveys to us, "*If anyone has material possessions and sees his brother in need but has no pity on him, how can the love of God be in him?"* (I John 3:17, NIV). Do you have the spirit of compassion?

When we are bitten by success, the poison can get into our blood stream and cause us to become proud. We forget about where we came from. God gave Solomon wisdom and knowledge, but he was bitten by success. He became poisoned. He allowed things to happen in the kingdom that should not have happened. David was bitten by success and he was almost totally poisoned when he called Bathsheba to his chamber, committed adultery with her, and caused her husband to be executed. The reign of his kingship caused him to think that he could endorse a man's death at the cost of his lustful desire. How many lives have been snatched by those in positions of power? David's heart almost became deaf to the voice of conviction, until God's mercy caused the prophet Nathan to speak a word of correction to him.

There are many men and women of God that have been bitten by success. They seek God for His blessing when their ministries are small and just beginning, but when they blossom, faithfulness to God is diminished, prayer time is stolen, and love for the brethren grows cold. When we esteem ourselves above others, and feel we are superior and invincible, we have been severely poisoned. We have not accomplished anything . . . God has allowed and given it all!

Swallow the Antidote

In Job 1:10, Satan told God that Job was serving him only because of the things that he was able to obtain and that if God would let Job down, Job would curse God. Not so . . . Job proved the devil wrong!

One of the most priceless things that one can have is the ability to love and to give. God is love. What people view as success is what society has labeled as success. Believers should not judge their success by the world's standards. A lot of the things that we deem success are superficial and do not last. What are things that last? Love, peace, joy and life—things that money can't buy. When the purpose of God is fulfilled in our lives, this is true success.

> *And he spake a parable unto them, saying, The ground of a certain rich man brought forth plentifully: And he thought within himself, saying, What shall I do, because I have no room where to bestow my fruits? And he said, This will I do: I will pull down my barns, and build greater; and there will I bestow all my fruits and my goods. And I will say to my soul, Soul, thou hast much goods laid up for many years; take thine ease, eat, drink, and be merry. But God said unto him, Thou fool, this night thy soul shall be required of thee: then whose shall those things be, which thou hast provided? So is he that layeth up treasure for himself, and is not rich toward God.*
> —Luke 12:16–21

Let us now look at the attitude of this individual. First, he thought within himself and began to display a behavior of selfishness. He never talks about seeking God concerning his wealth, nor reaching out to others, but he becomes poisoned by his gain. He became lifted up in pride concerning his worldly possessions and never took thought of life after death. How often do we ignore this point of view. That is, whatever we possess in this life really has no benefit to us when we are dead. I don't believe that Jesus had a problem with what the individual had accumulated, but He had a problem with his attitude. This lesson was geared toward those who would gain success through their material possessions. We should focus more on what it takes to gain eternal life and not be lifted up in the here and now.

To whom much is given, much is required. How do you keep from becoming poisoned? By giving and by sharing. We must not allow "things" (our looks, college degree, the family we've been raised in, job promotions) to go to our head, even if we are meeting all of the goals that we have set for ourselves. Without God, we are not successful. If we're not serving the purpose for which God created us, then we are truly unsuccessful. Notice, in the above passage of scripture the problem wasn't that the rich man gained a bountiful harvest, the problem was that he wanted to keep it all to himself. He did not understand that the reason he was blessed was so that he could be a blessing ". . . *And he said unto them, Take heed, and beware of covetousness: for a man's life consisteth not in the abundance of the things which he possesseth*" (Lk. 12:15).

> *And, behold, one came and said unto him, Good Master, what good thing shall I do, that I may have eternal life? And he said unto him, Why callest thou me good? there is none good but one, that is, God: but if thou wilt enter into life, keep the commandments. He saith unto him, Which? Jesus said, Thou shalt do no murder, Thou shalt not commit adultery, Thou shalt not steal, Thou shalt not bear false witness, Honour thy father and thy mother: and, Thou shalt love thy neighbour as thyself. The young man saith unto him, All these things have I kept from my youth up: what lack I yet? Jesus said unto him, If thou wilt be perfect, go and sell that thou hast, and give to the poor, and thou shalt have treasure in heaven: and come and follow me. But when the young man heard that saying, he went away sorrowful: for he had great possessions. Then said Jesus unto his disciples, Verily I say unto you, That a rich man shall hardly enter into the kingdom of heaven. And again I say unto you, It is easier for a camel to go through the eye of a needle, than for a rich man to enter into the kingdom of God. When his disciples heard it, they were exceedingly amazed, saying, Who then can be saved? But Jesus beheld them, and said unto them, With men this is impossible; but with God all things are possible.*
> —Matthew 19:16–26

I don't think the definition of success should be changed, but as we are blessed with success our attitude should be changed. The rich young ruler confronted Jesus and asked Him what he needed to do to be saved. Jesus told him that he should sell all that he had and give to the poor. We have to define the attitude that goes behind success. People have to maintain the right state of mind. Staying balanced is important. One can stay balanced by giving, by obedience, by service, and by sacrifice. *To whom much is given much is required.* While we desire success, we must commit to being responsible and accountable to the Spirit when the blessings come. When God invests blessings into our lives, they are not only for us to enjoy. He expects a return on His investment.

When people accumulate material possessions, it's easy to get caught up in a spirit of pride. They take on the "I got mine, now you get yours" mentality. Those with less money and possessions tend to share more than those people who have more to give. The Bible says that in the last days, men will be lovers of pleasures more than lovers of God. And this biblical prediction has come true. It's God's desire that you succeed, but as you succeed, commit to maintaining a humble spirit. Don't become poisoned. Remember, you are blessed to be a blessing.

CHAPTER SIX

Bit by Disease

Contracting a disease is a major concern throughout the world, particularly in this era of time where terrorism is a major issue. We hear alarming health threats across the news everyday. There is concern that deadly diseases such as smallpox or ebola will make their way into society and become uncontrollable. On another level, the nation is faced with finding a cure for diseases like diabetes, heart disease and cancer. Yet, for centuries, the attempt has been unsuccessful. It doesn't matter where you are or who you are, the reality of the effects of such diseases will get your attention.

Disease is just what it is: ***Dis-Ease.*** Anything that has the capability of overtaking you to the degree that you are affected and *controlled* by its symptoms is a disease. It doesn't necessarily always have to be physical, it can be spiritual, psychological, social or economical. Gambling, impulsive uncontrollable behavior, poverty, drinking, drug addiction and smoking are all types of diseases. They carry poisons that *can* affect your entire being. You don't have to be poisoned by disease just because you've been bitten by disease.

What You Don't Know Can Hurt You

There are many diseases that are silent killers and can poison us if they are not treated properly. Not only can a disease poison us physically, but the poison can also be spiritual. *"The spirit of a man will sustain his infirmity, but a wounded spirit who can bear?"* (Prov. 18:14). When you are committed and connected to God, there is strength inside your spirit. When you don't know the legal rights that you possess as a child of God, the enemy will use your ignorance against you every time. Not only did Jesus pay for our spiritual healing on Calvary, but also our mental, physical and emotional healing as well, *"By whose stripes ye were healed"* (I Pet. 2:24). You must know this and embrace what the Word of God says rather than the negative reports you receive from other sources. Again, remember that being poisoned starts at the place of incision. To counteract the venom, there must be an antidote within that's more powerful than the disease you're facing without. The antidote is the word of God.

> *For the word of God is living and active. Sharper than any double-edged sword, it penetrates even to dividing soul and spirit, joints and marrow; it judges the thoughts and attitudes of the heart.*
> —Hebrews 4:12, NIV

> *He was wounded for our transgressions, he was bruised for our iniquities: the chastisement of our peace was upon him and with his stripes we are healed. . . . Yet, it pleased the Lord to bruise Him: he hath put him to grief; when thou shalt make his soul an offering for sin, he shall see his seed, he shall prolong his days, and the pleasure of the Lord shall prosper in his hand.*
> —Isaiah 53:5,10

> *Bless the Lord, O my soul: and all that is within me, bless his holy name. Bless the Lord, O my soul, and forget not all his benefits: Who forgiveth all thine iniquities; who healeth* **all thy diseases.** *Who redeemeth thy life from destruction; who crowneth thee with lovingkindness and tender mercies.*
> —Psalm 103:1–4

The Word of God keeps us from being poisoned both *naturally* and *spiritually*. Not all diseases are fatal, but they can poison your mind, your spirit, your heart, your direction, and even your will to live. The key is to apply the Word of God at the onset of the attack. Allow it to serve as an anchor and stability to your soul. When we allow the Word of God to overtake us and not the disease, then poison doesn't go through our system, faith does.

It's All in the Mind

Your mind is one of the most powerful tools that God has given to you. It has the ability to imagine, to think, to conceal hidden secrets, or to cause your tongue to expose information. Even the mobility of your body is determined by the operation of your brain which makes up a part of your mind. In Genesis 11:6 we see the power of the imagination at work. When people are in unity of thought and speech, nothing that they imagine to do will be restrained from them. The images that you erect in your mind can eventually become a reality.

Due to the severity of certain medical conditions, many people receive death sentences pronounced over their lives like, "You have six months to live," "You'll never be able to function normally," "You will be on this medication for the rest of your life." The initial shock of news like this can cause the mind to wage mental battles developing strongholds with images of death, funeral processions, and gloom. The bite is intense and the fangs will try to lock themselves into your imagination. But, what does God have to say about the matter. In the first chapter of the book of John, we find that in Him (Jesus) was life. As long as you are in Him and He is in you, you have His life flowing through you. However, your imagination, or rather your mental faculties, must not be controlled by this world but be transformed by the renewing of your mind. There will always be a battle waging between your ears, but the good news is that you have an option. Yes, you have an option as to what you will think and what you will not think. What you will believe versus what you will not believe. You possess the power to think what you want to think. Even if the devil interjects thoughts into your mind, don't agree with them and allow them to fester in your mentality building a home to reside in. LET this mind be in you which was in Christ Jesus. Remember it's not the bite that kills, but it's the poison that comes with the bite.

Don't Be Overtaken

When bit by a disease, the poison can cause you to give up hope and develop a death mentality. I often say, I may experience the symptoms, but I don't have the disease. You could allow it to overtake your life, which is exactly what the enemy wants you to do. Being bitten by a disease does not mean that you have a death warrant. You could have an incurable disease or disability and still be a productive individual in society. It's all in your attitude and your faith. I'm reminded of a powerful testimony of a woman who was hospitalized due to a paralyzing stroke. She didn't allow her condition to hinder her. She said, "Lord, if I could raise one finger, I would wave it in praise to you." Before she knew it, she was waving her hand before the Lord. She continued praising God, saying, "Lord, if I could pat my foot I could praise you with my foot." Before she knew it, she was moving her feet in praise to the Lord. God worked a complete miracle for that woman and she walked out of the hospital. You see, you must use everything you *can* to praise God!

In Special Olympics, people with physical disabilities come together to compete against one another in sporting events. If they allowed themselves to become poisoned by their diseases or physical limitations, they wouldn't have a mind or desire to participate. Even though you may have a disease, you can't sit back and wait for the disease to overtake you. You still have a life to live. You have to make the most of it and serve the purpose for which God created you. The disease could be a part of that purpose. Nothing will happen without God allowing it to.

Fight the Good Fight of Faith

One question that many ask themselves when facing disease is, "Do I have enough faith to get through this storm?" We must be careful that we don't have *faith* in *faith*, but rather *faith in God*. Many precious people think that their confession alone will usher them into healing. Although confession is very important and has its place in the healing process, we must make sure that we are placing our faith in the right position, and that is in Jesus. When we have faith in faith, it often opens the door to denial, which will never allow you to receive the true benefits of healing. For example, pain is very real. The agony and intensity of pain that some diseases carry can literally cause a person to give up hope. Believing God has nothing to do with denying pain, but rather understanding that although the pain may exist, Jesus experienced the agony of pain for you on Calvary. Therefore, your faith lies in what the Word of God says because the Word declares that you have been *redeemed*, set free and ransomed from the disease because of the work that Christ Jesus has done. Therefore, you can take authority over the pain that you're experiencing. It must leave because it has no ownership over your body. Your proclamation of faith does not reside in saying, "No, I'm not in pain," when you feel like you've been run over by a freight train, but rather your response should be, "Although I may be experiencing pain, I believe that Jesus has taken my pain on Calvary, and I am persuaded that I am healed." As we trace men and women of the Bible we find that they had great testimonies of faith, yet, they went through difficult situations. Job was a man that was stricken with disease by the devil, but he overcame. Even Abraham was noted as the Father of faith—not for his *ability*, but simply because he believed God regardless of what the situation looked like. We must understand that there are levels of faith, yet faith will only be increased as we use it. As Abraham approached the mount to slay his son of promise—Isaac—at the command of the Lord, he had no doubt that he and Isaac would both return from the mount together (Gen. 22:5; Heb. 11:19). He knew that even if Isaac died, God was able to raise him from the dead and *received* him in an image (Heb. 11:17–18). He had already placed his faith in the fact that he would return from the mount with his son alive. The moment you *receive* in your spirit what God has already done whether you see or feel the manifestation, you will have what you are believing God for. Jesus said, *"all things are possible to him that believeth,"* but we must be sure that our belief is aimed in the right direction . . . *Have faith in God*. Faith should never be self-centered. God honors *faith* because *faith* honors Him. As we walk through the gospels with Jesus, we hear Him ask questions like, *"Where is your faith?"* Where is your faith today? Does it lie in your ability to quote scriptures ? Does it lie in your regular church attendance? Or is your faith buried in the Creator, the King of Kings and Lord of Lords, your Rock, your Shelter and your Deliverer . . . Jesus Christ the Lord.

Do You See What I See

If you follow the story of Job closely, you'll find that Job gained an awesome revelation of God during the course of his illness. Who would have thought that this powerful man of God, who the Bible called perfect, would be afflicted with a horrible disease. After all, he had everything going for him, he had favor, he was rich, he owned a lot of land, and he was a person who spent time with God. A true worshipper! Yet, he suffered affliction. You may be reading this book right now and suffering with an ailment, wondering, *God why am I going through this, I've walked with you all my life*. God knew that Job would not curse him. Although Satan gave many attempts to destroy Job's confidence in his God, Job never lost his godly integrity. Don't lose your godly integrity. Sometimes miracles come instantaneously, sometimes they don't, but they all come in God's timing. Job's words to God in the end were: *"I have uttered that which I understood not. . . . I have heard of thee by the hearing of the ear, but now mine eye seeth thee"* (Job 42:3,5). How far do your eyes see? God's plan is so far beyond our temporal human vision. Lazarus was dead four days before Jesus raised him from the dead. Jesus had supernatural insight; He saw life beyond the grave. When we give God our faith with any sickness, we must rest in His sovereignty. When Moses was faced with one of the most important assignments of his life, he asked God, *"Who shall I say sent me?"* The all powerful God said, *"Tell Pharaoh I AM that I AM sent you."* God wants you to understand that he is your all and all. If you need a miracle, He says, *"I AM your miracle."* If you need a physician, He says, *"I AM your physician."* If your disease is fatal, He says, *"I AM the resurrection and the life." "I AM whatever you need."* He asks the question to you, "Do you see what I see? I AM the I AM."

SPIRITUAL DISEASE

Some people attend church only on Sundays, but will go to work five days a week. Which is more important? Not praying for seven days can make one weak and cause your spiritual immune system to become infected. Some can be bitten by a spiritual fever. It could cause us to lose our spiritual appetite and not have a hunger for the things of God. Here are some spiritual diseases in the church: pride, hatred, bigotry, spouses who won't submit to one another, and children who are rebellious against their parents. When you are poisoned, you are not effective or productive. Poison contaminates your system. In the natural, you're not able to give blood when you are poisoned. Life is in the blood. Experts can tell when you have certain diseases by testing your blood. It's all in the blood.

There are pastors and preachers who feel superior over the people in their congregation. God has given them a position, but for some, success becomes a disease. Disease can affect everyone, but we cannot allow ourselves to become poisoned. We have to realize what the disease can and will do to us. The Lord can heal us of all spiritual and natural diseases. One purpose of the blood of Jesus is to heal *all* manner of sickness. If you have a disease, go to God for deliverance.

The conclusion of the matter is this: disease all started with man's failure to obey the commandments of God. We must conclude that as long as we live in this fallen world disease will be present in the earth. Some diseases are a product of sins. God has made provision for our healing and deliverance. There are many scriptures where Jesus informed individuals after they received their miracle to "go and sin no more." Also, there were times that He stated that the manifested miracle was for the glory of God. We must understand that in spite of disease originating from the sins of Adam and Eve, all diseases are not associated with our sins. First things first: when approaching your sickness you must search your heart, making sure that there is no sin or disobedience against the Word of God. If there is, repentance must first be proclaimed. Afterward you can go to God on your behalf. The next example of sickness can be seen with the friends of Jesus: Mary, Martha and Lazarus. When Lazarus became sick unto death and even died, Jesus proclaimed that the sickness was not unto death, but for the glory of God. Although, Lazarus died, what mattered most was that Jesus said it was for the glory of God. You may be sick and it may seem as if God was unfair, but always remember, God is still in control. For Paul said as a believer, "to be absent from the body is to be present with the Lord." He also stated that to live is Christ, but to die is gain. Therefore, you can't lose!

CHAPTER SEVEN

Bit by Relationships

It's difficult to get anywhere in life without the help of someone else. Have you ever been in unfamiliar territory and suddenly found yourself lost with no clue as to which direction was north, south, east, or west? What did you do? You asked somebody for directions, right? Well, thank God you did, otherwise you probably would have continued on the wrong path. The fact is people need people. In the beginning, the majestic power of God was displayed so beautifully in everything that He created. God said let there be light and that was good, the waters were good, even the sea monsters and the wing birds were admirable in God's eyes, but there was one thing in the picture that was *not good*. *"It is not good that man should be alone"* (Gen. 2:18). Alone simply means that you are all one and you're without anything or anyone else. According to God, this is *not good* or admirable in His eyes. For all those who shout the wonderful testimonies of, "I've got Jesus and I don't need anybody else," here's an eye opener, you need Jesus, but you need people, too. Think about the body of Christ. Does it not consist of *many* believers that fulfill different functions, but are part of one beautiful unit? What about the Apostolic Ministry? Jesus didn't entrust it to the hands of one man, but many.

The truth is that it's difficult to accomplish much in life without the right connections. Good relationships must be cultivated with the love that comes from heaven. There are many types of relationships—mother-father, brother-sister, grandparents, husband-wife, and extended family. Unfortunately, many of us have been bitten by bad relationships with our parents, children, spouses, or friends and have experienced the nasty lick of bitterness, hurt, broken fellowship, and sometimes even the poison of unforgiveness. There can be so many negative issues in relationships. If we accept the poisons that come with these bad experiences, we will never receive the benefits of relationships on the level that God intended them to be. In fact, if we are not careful, we will allow one bad relationship to become a permanent stone for building new ones. If you're a good architect, you'll always build with the chief cornerstone, Jesus. All relationships must have a balance. They must be built upon the Word of God. If it's not built upon the Word of God, it will not survive. If it's not stable, it will be poisoned. There will be no humbling of oneself. There will be no love or compassion.

First Things First

Any relationship you have, whether it's with your mother, your pastor, or even your neighbor, is a reflection of your relationship with God. How do you relate to God? Are you whimsical, do you love Him sometimes, but not at all times? Are you a finicky praiser or do you bless the Lord at all times? Do you know what the first commandment was?—No, it wasn't "Thou shalt not steal" or " kill," but it was something much deeper than that. It had to do with LOVE.

> *Jesus said unto him, Thou shalt love the Lord thy God with all thy heart, and with all thy soul, and with all thy mind. This is the first and great commandment. And the second is like unto it, Thou shalt love thy neighbour as thyself. On these two commandments hang all the law and the prophets.*
>
> —Matthew 22:37–40

You will never be able to truly cultivate a good relationship if you don't know how to love. "Greater love has no one than this, that he lay down his life for his friends" (John 15:13). Now God is not only concerned with the way you love Him but, He is concerned about the way you love yourself and others. Men and women must come to grips with the fact that their relationship with God will affect their relationship with other people. A strong, unique, and unshakable relationship with God is the most important relationship that you can have. Isn't it wonderful to know that as we spend time fellowshipping with Him, we learn His voice, His ways, and embrace Him in an intimate way.

As we come to know Him, we actually learn more about ourselves. Now this could be a true challenge. Sometimes God has to shape us by cutting away the parts that aren't like Him. Then He molds us by engrafting more of His character into our character so that we can display the fruits of the Spirit—love, joy, peace, longsuffering, goodness, kindness, patience, faithfulness, and temperance. Go ahead and admit it. Is your fruit tree barren? Well, don't feel bad. Always remember fruit is not manufactured. It is produced and production is a process. Good relationships are based upon how we relate to God and how we come to grips with who we are. It is important that you know who you are and are confident in your distinction.

Learn how to develop a relationship with yourself. What do you like? Are you aggressive? Would you rather remain quiet or do you like to talk? Who are you? Don't always look for someone else to make you happy or validate your existence. You must realize that you are a valuable treasure and what you have to offer is priceless. God allows us to build a strong spiritual relationship with Him so that we are equipped to help others. But, it's difficult to do this if you don't know who you are. After all, we are fishers of men. Being able to help someone find himself or herself spiritually produces a great reward and inward fulfillment.

LOVE is the antidote to the poisons that many of us face when it comes to relationships. If ever you're in doubt about your love walk, just check the definition. We must choose to walk in love.

> *Love endures long and is patient and kind; love never is envious nor boils over with jealousy, is not boastful or vainglorious, does not display itself haughtily. It is not conceited (arrogant and inflated with pride); it is not rude (unmannerly) and does not act unbecomingly. Love (God's love in us) does not insist on its own rights or its own way, for it is not self-seeking; it is not touchy or fretful or resentful; it takes no account of the evil done to it [it pays no attention to a suffered wrong]. It does not rejoice at injustice and unrighteousness, but rejoices when right and truth prevail. Love bears up under anything and everything that comes, is ever ready to believe the best of every person, its hopes are fadeless under all circumstances, and it endures everything [without weakening]. Love never fails [never fades out or becomes obsolete or comes to an end].*
>
> —I Corinthians 13:4–8, AMP.

When Love's Not So Easy

It's easy to give and receive love when you are loved, but what about when you are rejected, wounded, or hurt by someone. Sometimes those nasty scars aren't so easy to heal. Just one wrong nudge and the wound pops open again. Matters of the heart are sensitive issues to deal with and it takes a skillful physician who knows how to properly suture a wound, even if the cut seems impossible to stitch. Yet, we know that with God—the Great Physician—all things are possible to them that believe, even emotional healing from relationships that have left us nearly shipwrecked. Jesus walked the road of rejection and hurt. His wounds were so deep that they literally went to the bone. So when you talk about what you've been through and who took you through the ringer, His experience supersedes any of your experiences by far. If He were never wounded, healing would not have been provided.

There are many scenarios that can breed rejection. Sometimes it comes from church members, friends, or even family members. One common scenario is the absence of a complete, healthy family unit. Not being raised in a conventional family environment with both parents can leave a negative impression on the heart of a child that can carry into adulthood, yielding a major imbalance. Many children are raised in single parent homes, others with their grandparents, and some have been adopted. They have been bitten by not being able to experience the joy of a relationship with their biological family. But they don't have to be poisoned.

Take for instance my life. I was adopted by my grandparents at five months old. The trauma and struggles of life caused my biological parents not to raise me. The situation placed tremendous tension on my siblings; gradually we drifted apart. Unfortunately, the gap of unfamiliarity between my biological parents, my siblings and myself widened. I didn't realize until later the value of being raised by my grandparents, the situation however, placed me in the awkward position of experiencing rejection. Of course, I didn't realize this until I entered school and faced the battleground of teasing children. "You live with your grandparents?" "Don't you have a real mommy and daddy?" Comments such as these made me question a lot of things, but thank God I wasn't poisoned. Look at me now, a man of God with an anointing upon my life! God has a way of setting you up in situations that will bring healing to you in the area of relationships, even rejection—if you allow Him to. Sometimes healing comes through people you encounter every day. They may be a little different than what you're used to dealing with. Perhaps they "work your nerves a bit." The key is staying submitted to God. Sometimes those "challenging" people are instruments that God uses to work things out of us that are not pleasing to Him. Once we agree to submit to God, we will better understand some of the situations we go through.

Jesus experienced the most powerful degree of rejection one could ever experience. Just think about being crucified by people who were familiar to you. The prophet Jeremiah and Joseph experienced rejection. Even though many rejected the Word of the Lord from the lips of Jeremiah, he still spoke out against the false prophets of his era. He had a relationship with his God and his relationship with the children of God was a reflection of his relationship with His heavenly Father (Jer. 23).

In the book of Genesis, Joseph experienced what I call severe rejection. Although God revealed to him through a dream that he would be elevated to a high place of authority and his family would bow before him, he had a horrible relationship with his brothers. He was different, and his difference caused him not to be accepted. His brothers were jealous of him. Joseph had tremendous favor with his father and Jacob openly expressed his favor by giving Joseph a coat of many colors. Of course this only intensified the tension between siblings. How familiar is this story? We see family rivalry on TV talk shows constantly. *"My parents like him better than me" . . . You're just too different" . . .* The passion of hatred rose in the hearts of Joseph's brothers to such a degree that they planned to kill him. It's amazing how many kill their loved ones over trivial matters, arguments that could have been avoided.

The Bible declares that in the last days, the *love* of many shall wax cold (Matt. 24:12). We see the manifestation of this prophecy fulfilled today. I don't believe Joseph was trying to be malicious in sharing the dream that God had given him, but perhaps his brothers were not in a place where they could receive and understand what God was truly speaking to Joseph, for the vision was only revealed in part and was for an appointed time. Joseph wanted them to know that God was going to use him. He would be the one to be a blessing to them. They could not accept what Joseph was saying because they could not see God's vision. So they sold him into bondage. He was taken into Egypt as a slave, lied on, thrown in the dungeon, and totally rejected by his brothers. But God delivered Joseph out of the dungeon. Joseph became the prime minister of Egypt. Even though he was bitten by his relationship with his brothers, he was not poisoned. He realized his purpose in life and his vision was fulfilled. He carried no unforgiveness or resentment in his heart against his brothers. How was he able to do that? He understood that God was in the midst of the situation all the time, even the things that appeared to be so hard to deal with. There are so many people who live life day to day with unforgiveness in their hearts. Let it go! A relationship with God will develop such an attitude that no matter what you go through, you can go through it successfully and lovingly.

God allows you to go through things for a divine purpose. Not just for your purpose, but for His purpose. So many times, we have the wrong attitude. Some "do unto others as they do unto them." Those who think and act this way invariably become poisoned. This is not the way we should think or feel. Even if someone does you wrong, you shouldn't allow that to affect the way you treat them. Yes, sometimes there are tears, sometimes there's silence. In Joseph's case, he wept. Being able to properly vent is important, but never should we harvest decay in our hearts until it produces a stench on our demeanor.

THE VALUE OF COMMITMENT

Commitment is a priceless treasure. So many relationships are built on flimsy ground and when difficulties hit, the relationship wavers with no anchor of stability, particularly in today's society where convenience is so common. Divorces are on a constant rise across the United States and in other countries. The passion and desire to become intimately involved with a person supercedes that value of true commitment and godly love.

The professional basketball player Ervin "Magic" Johnson admitted that he contracted AIDS. He was married when he publicly announced this information. In some cases, such an acknowledgement would have destroyed his marriage and his career. His wife could have packed her bags and left, but she stood by her husband. She stayed by his side and didn't allow the disease or the fact that he had been unfaithful to poison or destroy their relationship. Instead, their commitment for one another became stronger and it even caused him to speak out against the awful disease. They did not allow the poison from the experience to consume their lives.

There are thousands of women who suffer both mental and physical anguish when a doctor discovers breast cancer or other diseases that affect their female organs. The only option is removal of the organ and a life without the fulfillment of bearing a child. What about men who have been devastated by prostate cancer and have lost vital organs? Yet, in spite of these terrible events, many husbands and wives *choose* to stay together and not allow these diseases to consume their lives.

Some parents suffer the pain of giving birth to deformed and handicapped children. However, they realize that the child is a gift from God. And their trust is in the sustaining power of the Almighty to enable them to endure and nurture that child in a relationship that displays the love of Christ. They have been bitten, but they are NOT poisoned.

The Boomerang Effect

The reality of life is that we may experience hurt, bruises, or maybe even wounds, but we don't have to be poisoned. You may have been hurt by people saying that they love you , but who never show it in their actions. Even though you have been bitten, there is one relationship that should remain solid as a rock, and that is your relationship with Jesus Christ. He will never fail you or give up on you. He loves us even when we are unlovable.

On this highway we call life, relationships come and go. Recognizing the traffic signals is a learning process and unfortunately, you will encounter a few fender benders along the way. But as you move forward, you'll learn the art and gain maturity through patience and practice. People come into our lives for different reasons, some for a moment, some a season, and some for a lifetime, but God is there for eternity. Realize that some people are on assignment from hell to destroy you, yet there are others who are sent by God to enlighten you. It's up to you to recognize which is which and maintain a balance of wisdom.

Often times, we base relationships on our expectations and anticipations. But they should be based on what we are willing to give, not just receive. Sometimes what we expect or anticipate from a relationship can place unnecessary pressure on the other person. Due to the weight of pressure, the *"rubber band"* of cohesiveness snaps, creating all sorts of negative emotions to deal with. The result is a cycle of disharmony, full of rifts, tension, and strife. Disappointment weaves itself into the world of what you thought would be a reality. Never allow your expectations to lie in an individual, because people are flesh, they are human—but God is eternal and He can fulfill every expectation that you have.

No relationship should be judged by experiences from the past. Many people enter new friendships with luggage that's filled with old, raggedy garments from yesterday's closet. Bad temperaments, ill communication habits, anger, resentment, jealousy, and the bag gets bigger and bigger. Don't bring yesterday into your future. Instead of discarding the luggage, they allow it to weigh both themselves down and those around them. Loving freely with open hands becomes a task because they're not willing to throw away the old and embrace the new. Learn to let go!

Resist the temptation to compare. Comparison is dangerous. Whether you're comparing the person with someone else, or simply an experience you've encountered, you will rob yourself of experiencing the beauty of the person for who they really are and you will never reap the benefits in which God designed the relationship to bring. When it comes to bad things you've encountered such as hurt, bitterness, or rejection, you must be careful not to allow yourself to superimpose an image from the past on those that are in your life for the present. Otherwise, you'll be caught in an echo of a boomerang effect, and what you experienced then, you'll experience again.

Let's develop true relationships that are unbreakable and inseparable. In I Samuel 18, David and Jonathan had a special bond of friendship, a covenant bond. Their souls were knit together. Jonathan loved David as his own soul. In spite of the fact that Jonathan's father, Saul, hated David, Jonathan didn't allow his father's attitude to poison his friendship with David. Many of our relationships should develop into a spiritual marriage, an unshakable bond, something that cannot be moved. We have all been created to be a blessing. As God blesses you, you are commissioned to bless others, not only financially, but even through your friendship. There are some people today who are starving for the love and attention of a true friend, and you can give them what they need. Continue doing what God has called you to do no matter how many times you have been bitten. Realize that God has made you who you are. Don't stray from that.

Prayer

Most gracious God, I ask you to heal me from the affects of past relationships that have not been productive and conducive to my betterment. I choose to forgive those that may have inflicted abuse—verbally, mentally, psychologically, and emotionally on me. I repent for anything that I have done to cause ill feelings to others. Help me to be more open to those you send into my life to help better me as an individual. As I commit my relationships, past, present and future, into your hands, I ask of you to lead and guide me by the power of your Spirit,to build relationships that are a reflection of your love. In Jesus' name. Amen.

You should now be prepared for any relationship that may come your way. You're a winner. You won't be defeated. Whatsoever you do shall prosper. There are people who need you and there are people who are in need of your friendship. Never tell someone that you don't need him or her, because we really need one another. You may not need them today, but you may need them tomorrow or next week.

Even if you have been bitten by relationships, you still know how to love, because God is love. Don't focus on your pain; focus on your power. Know that the Lord is your shepherd and He will lead you. Realize that your relationship with God can make you better than you have ever been.

CHAPTER EIGHT

Bit by Infidelity and Divorce

It's almost time for the big event. She's taken time to prepare herself in a stunning white dress that glistens as she walks. Her nails are perfect and there's not a hair out of place as she walks the walk of honor down the aisle to meet her groom — a strong, handsome man suited in a tux fit for a king. He has vision, ambition, character, and love for his new bride. They've made plans to work toward a happy future. Together they interlock hands facing the minister repeating vows of marriage—a covenant of love and consecration to God and one another.

Five years later they are divorced. What happened to break the Kodak moment? The claws of infidelity crept into their secret place of intimacy, ripping away the purity and sacredness of their vow. Infidelity simply put is *unfaithfulness*, the violation of the marriage covenant by adultery. The word *infidelity* stems from the root word infidel (one who does not believe in the inspiration of the scriptures or the supernatural origin of Christianity). A man who will not take care of his family is worse than an infidel. *"But if any provide not for his own, and specially for those of his own house, he hath denied the faith, and is worse than an infidel"* (I Tim. 5:8).

A marriage between husband and wife is an earthly representation of the awesome oneness between Christ and the church. In Ephesians 5, Paul writes that this is a great mystery. The union that we have with our Lord and Savior is supernatural. Without question Satan will try to destroy anything that's a representation of the love that Christ has for His church. Infidelity is one of the malicious devices he uses to accomplish this mission. What God hath joined together let not man put asunder. When adultery occurs in the life of a married couple, the Creator's beautiful miracle of two separate distinct pieces becoming one is ripped apart by an impostor. *"Wherefore they are no more twain, but one flesh. What therefore God hath joined together, let not man put asunder"* (Matt. 19:6).

Why do men and women cheat? Certainly there are demonic spirits on assignment to destroy marriages; they are masked in enticing flesh suits that appeal to the eye and body. Just a thought will push buttons that send off sirens in the emotional realm that pervert simple admiration into a conception of lustful imaginations. What was conceived becomes a reality. It's the spirit of Delilah sifting away the strength of those she entices.

There are a few other reasons to consider: lack of self-respect, a lack of understanding, lack of communication, and lack of fulfillment. A few moments of thrill can result in a lifetime of struggles, pain and heartaches. The torture of a severed family, broken trust between children and the unbelievable strain of having to rebuild character and credibility to those that have been let down could take more than a lifetime to correct. Sometimes the damage is not reparable. We know that many diseases are transmitted because of infidelity. These diseases spread like a plague with no regard for who is affected, even if it's the innocent spouse that has no knowledge or control of what they are being exposed to. Some cheat on their spouse because they do not take the time to think about the consequences of their impulsive sexual behavior. Sometimes it's the spouse who is the contributing factor to his or her mate's actions of infidelity. Many in the church today don't honor the marriage covenant at all. They don't value the covenant. *"Let the husband render unto the wife due benevolence: and likewise also the wife unto the husband, The wife hath not power of her own body, but the husband: and likewise also the husband hath not power of his own body, but the wife"* (I Cor. 7:3–4).

You may feel that your spouse has not given you love or attention and you may be right in your way of thinking. But this does not give you the right to hurt them by being unfaithful. Many times the victim becomes the villain. For example, a man cheats on his wife and the wife turns around and cheats on her husband thinking she can get even. This act can be defined as a type of transferring of spirits. *"What? know ye not that he which is joined to an harlot is one body? for two, saith he, shall be one flesh"* (I Cor. 6:16). The forbidden act of infidelity now has transpired into something more. A certain curse has been released over the household. Infidelity not only affects the offended spouse, but the children as well. Many have taken the wrong direction. They've been bitten, and have allowed Satan to use them as instruments to spread poison. As a result, there are broken hearts, shattered dreams, and even lost lives. Some have even committed suicide and murder for revenge. The question is asked, "Why?" "How could he or she say that they love me and treat me this way?" "How could he or she say that they love me, but cheat on me and my children?"

One of the greatest illustrations of infidelity in the Bible is that of the prophet Hosea and his adulterous wife, Gomer, whom he married at the instruction of the Lord. Hosea's love for Gomer was a reflection of God's love for backslidden Israel. God instructed Hosea to love Gomer with the love of the Lord and bring her back home although she was yet in an adulterous lifestyle (Hos. 3). The account of these two people can be viewed as a symbolic representation of God's love for His people. The scripture says that God is married to the backslider. Many times we have gone about doing what we wanted to do. God has been hurt by our infidelity. We, His children, after making marriage vows to Him, have not been faithful.

Infidelity is one of the biggest causes of broken marriages today. Many marriages lack love, respect, compassion, concern, and trust. Do we marry looking for happiness in another individual or do we marry because of love? Do we develop good, solid relationships, or are they simply based on the physical? Once the physical is experienced, what's left? Nothing, no substance and no foundation to build upon because the moment of fleshly pleasures has been fulfilled, so the reason for marriage has been fulfilled and there's no need for continued pursuit with the individual.

It Becomes Spiritual

Infidelity is generally associated with married people. This act is done when one does not realize that marriage is an agreement that has not only been made with man or woman, but also with God. Can one be forgiven? Yes, if they ask for forgiveness and truly repent. But, remember, only godly sorrow can work true repentance. Can one be freed of that spirit? Yes, because Jesus has paid the price for all. When we read the story of King David and Bathsheba, who was not his wife (II Sam. 11:3–15), we can see clearly how infidelity can cause one to do things that not only hurt and destroy oneself, but others as well. For example, Bathsheba conceived a child which was not her husband Uriah's, but David's. When she told David, he immediately went into action by attempting to deceive Uriah to sleep with Bathsheba. But because it was a time of war, Uriah was so dedicated to the cause that he would not. So, David had him put on the front line and he was killed. Even though the first child died, we can still see how the effects of this sinful affair affected David and Bathsheba's son, King Solomon, later on in life. Sometimes the spirit of adultery will follow a family line. The iniquity of the forefathers invites familiar spirits into the bloodline. It's important, for the sake of deliverance that the spirit of adultery is dealt with. Face the fact, if the problem exists.

- ❖ Commit yourself to consistent prayer and fasting.
- ❖ Entreat God for His forgiveness, deliverance and cleansing. "What can wash away my sins, nothing but the blood of Jesus" This comes through true repentance.
- ❖ Renew your mind in the Word of God; this will build strong mental structure and eradicate the strongholds of the enemy.
- ❖ Ask for grace and protection from God to guard against temptation.
- ❖ Submit yourself to counseling from your pastor or a strong spiritual leader.
- ❖ Be honest with yourself and your mate.
- ❖ Forgive.

It is necessary for married couples to evaluate their marriages. Ask the question, "How can I better my marriage?" The Apostle Paul said, *"But he that is married careth for the things that are of the world, how he may please his wife. There is difference also between a wife and a virgin. The unmarried woman careth for the things of the Lord, that she may be holy both in body and in spirit: but she that is married careth for the things of the world, how she may please her husband"* (I Cor. 7:33–34). A married person should be concerned about how he or she can please their mate. Is that what we really do? Do we really minister to our husbands and wives or are we really trying to please ourselves? And when we're not pleased, do we search for pleasure with someone else?

Having a selfish attitude or selfish disposition can cause us to not realize the need for love or the need to show love. Our purpose for living is to desire to be more like Jesus. *"For God so loved the world that he gave . . ."* (John 3:16). We must give in our marriages. We must give of our time, our love, and we must sacrifice for one another. What's love got to do with it? Love has everything to do with who we are and what we are. How wonderful it is to think about Christ and how He died for us. How He loved us so much that He left his throne in Glory to bring to us redemption. He could have stayed in heaven with the splendor, the walls of jasper, the pearly gates, and golden streets. But He came to earth to be the perfect sacrifice, an example for all humanity. If a man cheats on his wife and leaves her, she must realize that she has been uniquely made, and not allow her pain to consume her. If a woman cheats on a man, he must realize that God loves him and that he also has been uniquely made, and should overcome. He should not hold himself responsible for what his spouse has done (or doesn't do). Stand your ground. You may be bitten, but you don't have to be poisoned. If you have cheated, look at the damage that you have done not only to your spouse and your children, but also to yourself. No one wins through infidelity.

If you are the villain, ask God to forgive you and deliver you from the bondage and the appetite of sexual sin because it's a dead-end street. If you are the victim, ask God to help you to overcome; seek God for specific instructions concerning your situation as it relates to your mate. Don't allow the enemy to poison your trust in God. He will deliver you. He will rescue you. If that man or woman does not want you, move on. You are not responsible for what anyone else does. Only for what you do. Therefore, it is vital for you to forgive, so that your heart can be free. Watch the hand of God manifest itself in your life. You will be able to help others. The Lord said that vengeance is His. Remember, it's not the bite that kills, but the poison. Things will get better if you only put your trust in God. There are many that will use scripture for divorce.

- ❖ Hardness of heart
- ❖ If the unbeliever departs
- ❖ Fornication or adultery

However, I feel that we should try all options to make marriage work. It has been noted statistically that fifty percent of all marriages end in divorce. Although the Bible gives us grounds for divorce, we must ask ourselves is it really the answer in *every* situation. It has been said that many violent crimes are a result of divorce. Not only are there violent crimes committed such as rape and murder, but the lives of the children are affected in so many ways through things like teenage pregnancy, feelings of rejection, or even drug abuse. Some children develop low self esteem because they feel as if they are the cause of their parent's divorce. Unfortunately, in most cases these children end up divorced themselves. It has always been the motive of the enemy to destroy the family structure which was ordained by God in the beginning. Many are poisoned and resort to multiple marriages to fulfill their fleshly desire. Thus, the divorce rate for second-time marriages is even higher than those of first-time marriages. This poison must be dealt with! We must obey the Word of God and have respect for His Word and one another. None of us are perfect and, yes, there are valid reasons for divorce. Yet, we must make the committment to get along, love, and forgive one another. We must not allow the enemy to cause us to disobey the Word of God prior to marriage. Some couples experiment with one another sexually prior to marriage. This poison is a product of disobedience and rebellion against the Word of God which gives Satan free course to attack the purity and sacredness of marriage. We must realize that we are made in God's image and likeness; therefore we must exhibit characteristics of holiness.

There are those that have been influenced by Hollywood, and even by some church leaders who display the attitude that it's okay if you're not satisfied or happy in marriage to exchange one mate for another. This type of thinking is totally contrary to the Word of God. A person does not have the right by God's standard to make a vow and not keep it. Ecclesiastes 5:5–6, clearly states, *"Better is it that thou shouldest not vow, than that thou shouldest vow and not pay. Suffer not thy mouth to cause thy flesh to sin; neither say thou before the angel, that it was an error: wherefore should God be angry at thy voice, and destroy the work of thine hands?"* Ask yourself these questions: "Is it worth it to cheat and cause all these problems, or have I done everything in my power to make things right?" No matter how we feel, we should want to be right in the sight of God.

Now, I'm open enough to know that there are some things that are simply unavoidable, but we should desire the blessings of God. For God says, He will not withhold any good thing from those who walk uprightly before Him. Therefore, we must maintain an attitude of obedience to God at all times in order to be truly delivered and healed from the pain of infidelity and divorce. These things can be very hurtful, but there is life after divorce. God can bless you abundantly through another marriage and heal your wounded children. If you are the violator of the marriage, God can forgive you and give you a new start. But, I must warn you it sometimes can be a difficult process.

Power can come from your pain if you will allow it to. Know that God is on your side and He will make a way. Just because your marriage may fail, it doesn't mean that you are a failure. You have to rise above it. That's why, as believers, it is important for those of you who are married and have been bitten by infidelity, by neglect, by adulterous affairs and abuse to understand that you don't have to be poisoned. You can conquer. You can stand. You are a winner! Stand even when you don't understand.

CHAPTER NINE

Bit by Deceit

Deceit is cunning, crafty and one of the most sophisticated weapons that Satan uses to fulfill his desire. It's almost transparent because unless you have discernment from the Holy Ghost, the Spirit of truth, you won't even recognize that it's there. To the natural eye or ear it appears to be truth, but when truth is revealed the victim comes to the realization that he has only been living in a world of *virtual* reality. We see deception at work in the very beginning when the serpent beguiled Eve.

> *Now the serpent was more subtle and crafty than any living creature of the field which the Lord God had made. And he [Satan] said to the woman, Can it really be that God has said, You shall not eat from every tree of the garden? And the woman said to the serpent, We may eat the fruit from the trees of the garden, Except the fruit from the tree which is in the middle of the garden. God has said, You shall not eat of it, neither shall you touch it, lest you die. But the serpent said to the woman, You shall not surely die, For God knows that in the day you eat of it your eyes will be opened, and you will be like God, knowing the difference between good and evil and blessing and calamity. And when the woman saw that the tree was good (suitable, pleasant) for food and that it was delightful to look at, and a tree to be desired in order to make one wise, she took of its fruit and ate; and she gave some also to her husband, and he ate.*
>
> —Genesis 3:1–6, Amp.

Satan is a deceiver, he's a skilled archer at using his arrows of deceit and those who have been wounded are victims of his deception. How did Satan trick Eve? Let's travel through the pages of the Word of God to see what happened. The first thing the enemy did was question Eve to see if she really knew what God's instructions were. "*And he said unto the woman, Yea, **hath** God said, Ye shall not eat of every tree of the garden.*" Notice, his question was an assault against the integrity of the Word of the Lord. We should never let anyone or anything cause us to question or doubt God's Word—no matter how we may feel or what we hear. Neither should we entertain the thoughts the enemy tries to inject into our minds. Reject them! His ultimate goal is to sift the knowledge of the truth out of you and replace it with a lie. He gave Eve part truth, but the rest was a lie. "*And the serpent said unto the woman, Ye shall not surely die: For God doth know that in the day ye eat thereof, then your eyes shall be opened, and ye shall be as gods, knowing good and evil.*" The truth was reasoned away. Strategically, other tactics were used against Eve and they were—the lust of the flesh, the lust of the eye, and the pride of life. She *saw* that the tree was good for food, pleasant to the *eyes*, and *desired* to make one wise. She was intrigued by the information she gained, persuaded, and then manipulated into action, so she and Adam ate fruit from the forbidden tree. But what she was told was a lie.

> *Why is my language not clear to you? Because you are unable to hear what I say. You belong to your father, the devil, and you want to carry out your father's desire. He was a murderer from the beginning, not holding to the truth, for there is no truth in him. When he lies, he speaks his native language, for he is a liar and the father of lies. Yet because I tell the truth, you do not believe me!*
>
> —John 8:43–45, NIV

The enemy's natural characteristic is lying. *Everything* that Satan says is composed of a lie. Sometimes it's not so easy to determine a lie, especially when it's masked in a familiar face. For Eve the face was that of a serpent. Sounds peculiar? Perhaps it wasn't an abnormal situation for her to have a conversation with a snake, the Bible never indicates that the scenario was out of order or uncommon; neither did it indicate that she was alarmed by the conversation. During the 1970s a preacher led many of his followers to their death by lacing their drinks with poison. He taught a false doctrine called *translation*—which meant that he and his followers would all die together. Who would think that a man who spoke of God, love, and compassion would lead his congregation to death and hell? He was a familiar face to those he killed.

As we near the coming of Christ we must be able in this end time to discern and guard against the spirit of deception. Today there are talk shows that encourage belief in psychics, spiritual mediums that contact the dead, and that tap into the demonic spiritual world (Deut. 18:10–11)—this is deception at one of its highest levels. Why? Because the hearers become captivated and intrigued, so therefore demonic spirits are very easily imparted into their lives. The Second Epistle of John lets us know that the spirit of the antichrist is a deceiver. Wake up, church, be on alert! It's time to covet earnestly the best gifts of the Spirit, so that we can be equipped for spiritual warfare and effectively stand against these demonic forces. The only thing that will counteract deception is the Spirit of Truth. We must be *filled* with the Spirit of Truth—the Holy Ghost, not simply knowing or being a student of the Word only, but allowing the Word to be a piercing two-edged sword cutting deep into our very souls, severing all darkness with the light of truth, for Jesus came full of grace and truth (John 1:14).

On a Personal Level

While you may think that the spirit of deception only operates on a large scale such as what happened with Eve, or in the above preacher's account, it's very plausible that you have been affected. Could it be possible that you have been deceived? All of us have been bitten by deceit in life at some point. Here's a simple example: "lying." We must realize that a lie is a lie whether it's termed as a "little white lie" or a "big lie." There is no difference. The scriptures unveil to us that Satan is not only a liar, but he's the father of lies. The foundation of any house of deceit is built on and with a lie. Many have surrendered to the will of the devil in the area of lying and in their own imagination. Not only are they deceived, but they are being used to deceive others. In Jeremiah 23 God rebuked false prophets that were leading his people astray.

> *I have heard what the prophets said, that prophesy lies in my name, saying, I have dreamed, I have dreamed. How long shall this be in the heart of the prophets that prophesy lies? Yea, they are prophets of the deceit of their own heart.*
>
> —Jeremiah 23:25–26

We must become balanced even when it comes to things we feel that God has spoken to us. It's important that we truly convey what God is saying and not words or visions from our *own* heart, for to convey the wrong message will not only deceive others, but will also cause them to err. The prophets in the above passage of scripture proclaimed words from their *own* imagination. Now this is a fine line, and false prophets in times of old and even many today have crossed it. The question may arise, "How does a person know when it's God and when it's not God?" The answer is simple, wait on the counsel of the Lord—spend time with Him, search your motive, know that God's Word is proven—He will always confirm His Word. And finally, any word of the Lord should be backed with scripture. The reality is that many are not aware that they are operating in deception. And of course, this is the art of the weapon; you don't know it's there until it's too late.

The Bible says that we can deceive ourselves by saying that we have no sin (I John 1:8). A person could even be deceived out of knowing God's purpose for their life by believing untrue things and convincing others that those things are true. *"For the time will come when they will not endure sound doctrine; but after their own lusts shall they heap to themselves teachers, having itching ears; And they shall turn away their ears from the truth, and shall be turned unto fables"* (II Tim. 4:3–4). Now we must realize that there is a difference between one who functions as a deceiver and a person who has simply been misled. A deceiver is one who is controlled by the spirit of deceit, whose hidden selfish motive is the driving force of his actions. For example, you may tell someone, "I love you, I care about you, and I will always be there for you," but if something out of your control happens, you may not be able to fulfill your commitment. This is altogether different from telling someone that you love them just to get them into bed to have sex with them. The world is full of people who have been bitten and poisoned by deceitful people like this. The tendency of saying what people want to hear can become habit forming. So many conversations lack truth and sincerity. God is looking for honest people. As the saying goes, *"honesty is the best policy."* No matter who the truth may hurt, God wants us to be honest with our fellow man. Don't yield to the spirit of deceit. People who have become deceitful have corrupt desires. In some cases demonic spirits have overtaken them. Lesbians marry men knowing that they have no desire for men. Homosexuals marry women knowing all along that it's only a cover-up. They know that true deliverance hasn't taken place in their lives, so they get married to make a public statement. Fornicators go from one sexual partner to another knowing that they have no intention of building a solid relationship that will lead to marriage. But people do these things because their hearts are deceitful. They have no concern or compassion for the feelings of others. It's totally contrary to the Word of God to have hidden agendas, even in friendships. Sometimes people embrace the friendship of others just so they can get ahead, or name drop to get to the their next destination in life. There's no genuine concern for the person they're supposedly befriending. Here's what the Bible speaks concerning the deceitfulness of the heart.

> *The heart is deceitful above all things, and desperately wicked: who can know it? I the L*ORD *search the heart, I try the reins, even to give every man according to his ways, and according to the fruit of his doings.*
> —Jeremiah 17:9–10

I feel that it is vital to tell people not to allow their emotions to control them, but to control their emotions by the power of the Holy Ghost. If you don't, you will become overwhelmed and gullible. You become open prey for those who are not sincere and who practice deceit. When you love a person, it should be hard knowing that you may have hurt them. We must become more aware of how we affect one another's lives. It is important to know yourself and to know your ways. Even if it hurts, practice honesty from A to Z. If you want honesty, you have to be honest. Don't allow the spirit of deceit to take root in your life. Bind its operation and cast it out in the name of Jesus. God has not called you to be a deceiver. He has called you to be led of the Spirit so that you can lead people to Calvary. In this end time the power of God must be manifested within our lives so that men and women can be drawn to the saving power of Jesus Christ. But we cannot accomplish this ministry if we're walking in deceit. If you have deceived someone, admit your wrong and ask for forgiveness. Deceit can be a difficult spirit to gain control over, but God can free your mind and your spirit.

It's amazing how many people are taught deceit. Many of us have been taught how to lie. The little white lies we use in our daily lives become examples to our children. Whether it's lying to a telemarketer to get them off of the phone, or telling someone they're dressed nicely to spare their feelings. We make excuses, telling people that God "understands" and that we aren't really lying or deceiving anyone. Is this deceit? Yes, it is. There is a fine line between deceit and what we call excuses. We must be aware of how we conduct ourselves.

The book of Matthew lets us know that because of the abundance of iniquity (lawlessness), the love of many will wax cold. This is why we must arm ourselves with the mind of Christ, for the mind is the house of thought and we must guard it. It's important that we manifest fruits of righteousness, so that our spirit will be clean before God and not manifest anything that is contrary to the nature or the attributes of God, for the enemy will thrive on these things and gain a foot hole in our lives. If we truly desire to live by the standards of God, we can, for we've been given the power and authority to do so. The Holy Ghost is supernatural within itself. One of the gifts of the Holy Ghost is discerning of spirits. This gift allows us to discern whether the spirit in operation is of God, the devil, or simply the flesh (man). The Holy Ghost gives us power to discern our own deceit as well as the deceit of others. It matters little if it is the deceitfulness of others or the deceitfulness of ourselves. We must guard our spirits against all types of poison.

When was the last time you were deceitful? We have all been guilty of it, or victims of it. Know that God has called His people to a much higher plateau of excellence, don't allow the forces of hell to dictate your life with antagonizing lies. A liar will not tarry in God's eyesight (Ps. 101:7). Manifestations of trickery and manipulation must not have place in the life of a believer. Expose these spirits! The spirit of deceit has been sent by the enemy to pave the way for the Antichrist. Sometimes deceit can be so deeply rooted that it could take years for a person to overcome the hurt. When some people have experienced this type of hurt, they stop coming to church, they quit praying, and they even cease to believe in and serve God. They have no desire to fellowship or to develop relationships with other believers. Those that have been poisoned by this sting must allow the Holy Ghost through prayer to heal them totally. It can be difficult to forgive those who have defiled you through deception. Unforgiveness is one of the most vicious poisons that can enter our systems. The Word of God can purge us and heal our broken hearts (II Tim. 2:15-21; Luke 4:18).

Deceit takes no prisoners—it captivates and destroys those who will allow it. It destroys commitment to God, relationships with those we love, and can even sift you out of eternal life. It caused Adam and Eve to disobey God's command which was the ultimate downfall of humanity as a whole. Deceit is a trick of the enemy and it causes us to separate ourselves from God, His law, and His way. It only takes a little poison to kill you and most of the time it's packaged in something that appeals to your carnal nature.

> *But [now] I am fearful, lest that even as the serpent beguiled Eve by his cunning, so your minds may be corrupted and seduced from wholehearted and sincere and pure devotion to Christ.*
> —II Corinthians 11:3, AMP.

Prayer

Most gracious God, I ask of you, Lord, to give me clarity of thought and understanding, to know that within my flesh dwelleth no good thing. My flesh is constantly warring against the Spirit. God I ask of you to help me walk in the Spirit so that I will not fulfill the lusts of the flesh. Enlighten my mind with truth so that deception will have no entrance in me. Help me not only to know your will for my life, but help me to walk in your will. Grace me to overcome the things of the past. I have been bitten but with your help, I will not be poisoned by deceit. I welcome the convicting power of the Holy Ghost to deal with me. In Jesus name, Amen.

CHAPTER TEN

Bit by Bad Choices

As we endeavor to look into the Word of God we can see where God has given humanity the ability to make choices. By this we are saying that He has given us a free will. What an awesome privilege! One scripture that reveals the importance of utilizing the power of choice effectively is Deuteronomy 30:19, *"I call heaven and earth to record this day against you, that I have set before you life and death, blessing and cursing: therefore **choose** life, that both thou and thy seed may live."* When God says choose life, He's not necessarily talking about living only. Life consists of more than just living; it consists of conduct, behavior, attitude, and even our choices — the choices that we make every day. Your choice can alter the destiny that God has planned for your life. It's important to understand that the question of unconditional eternal security has an answer, and the answer is that our future depends largely on the path *we choose*. What I mean by this statement is that there are many debates over the fact that God makes all choices for us, regardless of how good or bad they are. There are many things we really don't understand about God and His sovereignty, but there is one thing that we must be clear on, and that is He doesn't want any to perish. He wants all to come to repentance that they might have eternal life. When we consider this important factor we must realize that because of God's love He has not created us to be puppets or robots. Yet, He has allowed us the ability to make choices. We can choose eternal life or choose death, choose heaven or choose hell. We can see this clearly in the life of Judas when he decided to betray the Lord for thirty pieces of silver. After realizing his mistake, neither life nor filthy lucre meant anything to him; even Jesus Himself said it would have been good if this man had never been born (Mark 14:21).

Think about the children of Israel and how often God dealt with them, showing His wondrous works, manifesting Himself as a pillar of fire by night and a pillar of cloud by day to lead and protect them, yet they still did things their own way. It was not the devil, but their own choice that brought many of them to damnation.

Cain's decision to yield to a heated moment of jealousy transformed him into a murderer. He violently took the life of his own blood brother. How repetitive is this scenario today, so many deaths are caused by outbursts of jealousy. Esau made the decision to give up his birthright for a morsel of food. The satisfaction of pacifying his flesh caused him to lose "the blessing." Countless blessings have been lost simply because of bad choices. Some choices could literally cost you your life. The choice that Lot's wife made to look back to Sodom and Gomorrah caused judgment to fall on her, a pillar of salt she became, poisoned. How many precious people have been paralyzed, not able to move forward in life, just because of one decision? They've been bitten and poisoned by bad choices.

Although all decisions that we make are not life threatening, it is important that we understand how to make good choices. Certainly determining which pair of socks to wear in the morning doesn't deserve our focused attention. But, there are millions of people in today's society that rehash important decisions they've made in the past and wish they could go back in time and live the moment again, choosing a different path. Sometimes when we think we're making a good choice, it could actually be a bad one. Where's the balance in this choice making thing?

We must realize that God is concerned about every part of our lives. His compassion enlarges itself over the vast areas and even reaches to the depths of the small things of life. Think about it. You are *fearfully and wonderfully made* (Ps. 139:14); even the very hairs of your head are numbered. He is concerned about your decisions. It's the manifest love of God that even allows us to have the privilege of making choices.

THE MANUFACTURER'S PARTS

Your existence is made up of more than what you see in the mirror every day. You're composed of body, soul, and spirit. Yet you are one person. The body or *soma* (Greek) is that part of you that goes back to the dust when you die. Many mistreat this part by choosing bad eating habits causing diseases like strokes, diabetes, and heart attacks. The soul or the *psuche* (Greek), which means the compilation of your mind, emotions, will, and intellect. This is the part of you that remembers, that feels happy or sad, and that makes decisions. But, there will be many times when your mind won't quite know what to think, because of the situation that lies at hand, your emotions may become offset and the ability to remain sober (alert) may be too difficult, but when you have the Holy Ghost, your spirit will already have the answer. If we had to depend solely on our mind to help us make decisions we would be most miserable.

The first strategic area that the enemy attacks is the mind, which houses many thoughts. Thoughts can originate within ourselves, we must understand that God has given us the ability to produce thoughts independently of any source, and these thoughts are defined as our own personal thoughts. For the book of Proverbs lets us know that as a man thinks in his heart so is he. Secondly, God can speak into our minds. The third method of thought is that which comes from the enemy. This is why the scripture tells us that we should let the same mind that is in Christ be in us (Phil.

2:1–9). This scripture is a must-read because it gives us the mind of Christ which is humility and obedience to the purpose of God.

God engrafts us with all the supernatural parts we need. The Greek word for spirit is *pneuma*. It's the life force or breath which causes you to function here on earth; it's God's given life, the ultimate life source. *"And the Lord God formed man of the dust of the ground, and **breathed** into his nostrils the **breath of life;** and man became a living soul"* (Gen. 2:7). Proverbs lets us know that the *"spirit of man is the candle of the Lord searching all the inward parts"* (Prov. 20:27). God can minister instruction to your spirit, for God is a Spirit and you were created in the image of God. *"I will bless the Lord, Who has given me counsel; yes, my heart instructs me in the night seasons"* (Ps. 16:7). Revelation knowledge is inside your spirit. Why? Because this is the part of you that is connected to God. *"... Shall we not much rather be in subjection unto the Father of spirits, and live?"* (Heb. 12:9). That is why it's so important that we are filled with the Holy Ghost and pray in the spirit constantly. When we don't know what to do the Holy Ghost will enlighten us because the *"Spirit also helpeth our infirmities"* (Rom. 8:26). Only through the Holy Ghost are we able to make the choices that are conducive to the plan, will and purpose of God.

There are three components that every believer must allow God to develop when it comes to making decisions and they are: wisdom, knowledge, and understanding. Now let us look at knowledge. Many individuals feel that they have all the knowledge that they need, but we must realize that there is a level of knowledge that only God can give. When we observe scripture, we see knowledge in so many different ways. For instance, when the Word of the Lord was spoken to Daniel he was told that knowledge would increase. This means that knowledge, which is simply the "state of knowing," shall be revealed to many concerning things to come. Understanding is the comprehensive ability to apply the knowledge you have gained. However, this is not enough, because our environment and the experiences we've faced in life can limit our understanding, for the Word of God tells us in all of our getting, we must get understanding. Yet, there is something deeper that we all need and that's wisdom. Wisdom is special discernment with which you are able to judge and deal with a situation. If we learn to embrace wisdom, a lot of bad choices will be alleviated. There is a grace that accompanies a person that is full of wisdom. They have the ability to make sound sober decisions without a struggle. There will be times when you will not know what to decide in a given situation, but through the gifting of His Spirit, God can give you a supernatural word of wisdom or a word of knowledge that will aide you in your decision process. But we must ask God to let these components operate continuously in our life. "*If any of you lack wisdom, let him ask of God that giveth to all men liberally, and upbraideth not; and it shall be given him*" (James 1:5).

Decisions, Decisions

Some people are afraid to make choices because they fear the outcome. In most instances, this is because they think their choice will cost them something. So they live a life of indecisiveness and are poisoned by an "I don't care" attitude. They live in fear due to past decisions that caused bad experiences. God gives not the spirit of fear, but He gives you power, love, and a sound mind. To have a sound mind, we must not allow ourselves to become poisoned, for many ask the question, "How did I end up back where I started? I promised myself that I would never do this again, I would never say this again, I would never act this way again." Discern the influence that caused you to make the choice in the first place. Take responsibility. You must realize beyond a shadow of a doubt that the choice you made was your choice, it wasn't predicated upon Satan or upon men or women, but it was a decision that you made on your own. So often bad decisions are made due to the emotions or the flesh and not by the direction of God. For example, some parents love their children so much that they allow them to do whatever they desire to do, just to appease them. It is important that parents train up their children in the admonition of the Lord and when they become older they will not depart from the way of the Lord. Parents should not allow their emotions to dictate discipline. Many children are raising themselves, and that's not God's plan. It is important as adults that we pray and seek the face of God for His divine direction for others. God has ordained parents to lead their children in the right direction. They are responsible not to raise them with negative overtones, criticism, and bad attitudes. A child's life depends on what is invested in them.

The best thing for you to do is to sit down and take a personal evaluation. Learn from your experiences. Be totally honest with yourself instead of making excuses for your bad choices. This is the only way to really become free from the things that have been birthed into existence through your bad choices. Sometimes, as believers, we don't want to see the negative part of ourselves for what and who we really are. We don't want to see how we have become a hindrance to ourselves and to others. Whatever it takes, we must come to grips with the fact that we may have affected our own destiny by our choice of words, attitude, and behavior. In evaluating experiences, ask yourself questions like, "How was I affected by that choice, by that decision?" "Was it helpful?" "Was it really worth it in the long run?" "Should I have held my peace?" or "Would it have been better to go to God in prayer?" Questions such as these will be very helpful the next time if you're willing to seek God in prayer and fasting before making major decisions.

When you are delivered from past bad choices and you receive your supernatural breakthrough, make sure that you don't take that same path again. I believe that we should approach all choices in faith knowing that the Spirit will help us with our infirmities. There's nothing wrong with praying and asking God for guidance, for the Bible says in Romans 8:26–27 that we don't even know what we should pray for as we ought, but the Holy Ghost makes intercession for us with groanings that cannot be uttered, and then it says, "He that searcheth the hearts knoweth what is the mind of the Spirit, because He maketh intercession for the saints according to the will of God." This verse lets us know that God is in control. He knows our end before our beginning, and our beginning before our end. Once we've sought God for guidance through prayer, Philippians 4:7 tells us that God will give us the peace that passeth all understanding.

> *Rejoice in the Lord always and again I say rejoice. Let your moderation be known unto man. The Lord is at hand. Be careful for nothing, but in everything by prayer and supplication with thanksgiving let your request be made unto God. And the peace of God, God's peace which passeth all understanding, shall keep your hearts and mind through Christ Jesus. Finally brethren, whatsoever things are true. Whatsoever things are honest. Whatsoever things are just. Whatsoever things are pure. Whatsoever things are lovely. Whatsoever things are of good report. If there be any virtue and if there be any praise, think on these things. Think on those things. These things which ye have both learned and received and heard and seen in me, do. And the God of peace shall be with you.*
>
> —Philippians 4: 4–9

You may have been bitten by bad choices, but you can make a new choice. As you seek God, you will discover that He has a way of taking away your sorrow, your pain, and even your guilt. The Bible says that old things are passed away, and behold all things have become brand new. Many times we quote this scripture, but do we really believe it. We have to believe this in spite of repeatedly being confronted with circumstances that remind you of your past failures and struggles. You have to be powerful and strong enough to know beyond a shadow of a doubt that you are delivered. If we could just learn how to trust God, and trust the fact that God is in us and that He is with us, we would be spared a lot of heartache. If we will just take the time to sit quietly before Him, He will give us instruction.

If we could only see a preview of things that are to come in our lives! God will show you a preview of your future if you ask Him. He showed Joseph fourteen years into the future, seven years of harvest and seven years of famine. What a blessing it is to know that God is faithful! The scripture says that He will not suffer us to be tempted above that we are able, but with that temptation, He will make a way of escape that we will be able to bear it. That's how good God is. He can take the temptation and make it work for our good. But we must allow Him to do this. We must allow Him to do what He wants to do with and in our lives, or we will not conquer and become mature believers.

In the book of Exodus, we read where the children of Israel had been bitten by so many adversities and hardships that they were willing to go back into Egypt and become slaves again to evil taskmasters. They were in unfamiliar territory and began to complain. In spite of God leading them, feeding them, and providing them with clothes that never wore out, many of them could not accept the change that God had ordained for them in fulfilling His purpose. So they turned their backs against Moses. Just because they could not see their way, it didn't mean that God wasn't on their side because it was Him that gave Moses the instruction when it came to leading His people out of bondage. What we must learn from this example is that God expects us to walk by faith and not by sight.

Some people have been bitten and are so contaminated that they cannot trust God. They lean to their own understanding and are not able to receive God's direction in their lives. When we choose to make choices based on our emotions or thought patterns, we may make bad choices. This is why we must lean toward the Spirit of God and not be so quick to judge based upon what we see or how we feel because things may turn out to be different later on. That's why so many end up in a mess because they didn't follow the leading of the Spirit in the beginning.

The Word of God makes it clear that all things work together for the good to them that love God, to them who are the called according to His purpose. The result of some choices that we feel are bad may not be as bad as the outlook. Sometimes we really don't realize this until we see the outcome.

CONCLUSION

Bit, But Not Poisoned

There are many direct attacks that the enemy uses against the people of God. Again, we must say that it's not the bite that kills or destroys, but the poison that comes with the bite. The last days are upon us and many are not equipped for the battles that the enemy is waging against all humanity. Although God will sometimes allow the enemy to attack us, this does not mean that the devil can steal our salvation, make us sin, or possess us against our will. We must understand that even as Jesus stood against him in the wilderness, we also can stand using the Word of God as our weapon of defense. When we deal with demonic forces we are dealing with the realm of the supernatural. Therefore, we must seek supernatural manifestations of the Holy Ghost to operate in and through our lives. In particular, using the gifts of the Spirit which enable us to discern the real purpose of the attacks we go through. The purpose of Satan's attacks is to steal, kill, and destroy. Consider the Apostle Paul, a Spirit-filled believer who experienced a thorn in his flesh that would not move. Even in the midst of this conflict, Paul gained a greater understanding and depth of God's grace, which caused him to know it was his weakest moments that paved the way for God's power to become perfected in his life.

> *Even if I should choose to boast, I would not be a fool, because I would be speaking the truth. But I refrain, so no one will think more of me than is warranted by what I do or say. To keep me from becoming conceited because of these surpassingly great revelations, there was given me a*

thorn in my flesh, a messenger of Satan, to torment me. Three times I pleaded with the Lord to take it away from me. But he said to me, "My grace is sufficient for you, for my power is made perfect in weakness." Therefore I will boast all the more gladly about my weaknesses, so that Christ's power may rest on me. That is why, for Christ's sake, I delight in weaknesses, in insults, in hardships, in persecutions, in difficulties. For when I am weak, then I am strong.

—II Corinthians 12:6–10, NIV

Each time a Christian is attacked, we should see it as an opportunity for God's power to be perfected in our lives. Sometimes we may not know exactly how or what to pray, but the Spirit of God will help our infirmities and make intercession for us so that the divine will and purpose of God will be done. Our confidence hinges on the fact that all things work together for good to them that love the Lord and to them who are the called according to His purpose. Here are seven deadly poisons that we must avoid: *hatred* is the most potent; the others are *pride*; *fear*, which manifests itself in several ways, one of the most common being insecurity; *lying*; *disobedience* and *rebellion* are twins; *bitterness* which opens the door to unforgiveness; and *unbelief*. When we think about these, we can clearly see how things that have been explained in this book such as infidelity, divorce, disease, inferiority, and failure can serve as avenues that spread these poisons. We must draw the conclusion that these poisons have to be avoided. How can we avoid them from entering our systems? With the proper antidotes.

Now that we've looked at the seven deadly poisons, we must realize that God has given us seven powerful antidotes to fight with. *LOVE* is one of the most potent antidotes, it will offset the ploy of Satan every time, especially when we are faced with personal attacks, for love is even stronger than death. In fact, *FAITH* works by love. We must have faith, for without it, we cannot please

God. *PRAYER* is powerful—it's your communication with God. It releases the flow of the anointing upon our lives from heaven to earth and from earth to heaven, for the scripture says, *"The effectual fervent prayer of a righteous man availeth much"* (James 5:16). Many battles start in the mind. We must have the antidote of *PEACE*, which will pass all understanding. After you have prayed with all prayer, then the peace of God will guard your heart and mind (Phil. 4:6–8). The *JOY* of the Lord is your strength in any situation you may face. *KINDNESS* is one of the fruits of the spirit. We need this fruit to manifest in every relationship we have. Finally, there's *TEMPERANCE* which helps us to be disciplined and controlled.

In spite of the things that have bitten us in life and may bite us, we must realize that God has made provision for us through His Word and we have been uniquely made for His glory and honor—no matter what we go through. We don't have to be poisoned! We must allow the Word of God to come alive in our lives and apply prayer, fasting, consecration, and dedication to the cause. I pray that you have become strengthened with all might in your inward man and you can truly say in the midst of your tests and trials, although I was bitten, I refused to be poisoned.

Audio/Video Materials by Dr. Robbi Warren

For purchase, please contact Robbi Warren Ministries or place order online.

Robbi Warren Ministries
P.O. Box 11951
Baltimore, MD 21207
(800) 478-4225
www.robbiwarrenministries.org

Cassettes

Bind Satan Before He Binds You	A002
Bit, But Not Poisoned	A008
Chosen	A005
Counter Attack	A024
Don't Say It Again	A019
Faith on Trial	A020
God Has Not Forgotten You	A017
I Won't Be Intimidated	A023
Is It Because There Is No God	A013
It Didn't Work	A010
It's Already Begun	A012
It's Time to Loose Yourself	A015
Leave It Behind	A021
Loose in the Fire	A014
Only Be Strong	A016
Spiritual Warfare	A-V-009
The Vision Will Speak for Itself	A011
What About the Soul	A025

CDs (Available)

Scriptures and Songs for Healing	C001
Audiovisual Materials	Upon Request

Videos

A Dangerous Assignment	V100-3
The Call	V104-3
It Shall Come to Pass	V107-3
Valuable But Not Invincible	V111-3
Let This Mind Be in You	V114-2
The Search Is On	V125-2
The Other Side of the Cross	V-A-127-2
It's Never About You, But About Him	V129-2
Can You Trust God?	V131-2
Unfinished Business	V133-1
Latter Rain Conference	V136-2
Opportunity of a Lifetime	V138-2
Healed But Not Whole	V141-3
Stand When You Don't Understand	V145-3
Let Him See Your Faith	V500
It's Just a Matter of Time	V502
The Vision Will Speak for Itself	V503
Same Clay, But Another Vessel	V504
The Devil's Assignment Has Been Canceled	V505
God Has Not Forgotten You	V506
Only Be Strong	V507
It's Just in the Plan	V509
I Won't Be Intimidated	V510

About the Author

Robbi Warren has devoted his life to teaching, preaching, and singing the gospel of Jesus Christ. He holds a Doctorate of Divinity from Eastern Bible College and is the founder of Robbi Warren Ministries, which is a multimedia ministry based out of Baltimore, Maryland. For over 25 years God has used him as an International Evangelist to stir the hearts of His people and through this ministry thousands have been healed, set free, and delivered. He can be seen on World Harvest Television (WHT–satellite); WATC-TV 57—Atlanta; KAZQ-TV 32—Albuquerque, Santa Fe and Central and North Central New Mexico; WACX TV 55/SCTBN Channel 9709 (TBN affiliate) Orlando, Daytona, Gainesville, Orange County, Sanford and surrounding areas; and the Word Network. These broadcasts are projected to reach millions of people throughout the U.S., South America, and Canada. Robbi's passion is to *win the lost at any cost* and he serves as a prophetic voice to the body of Christ, sounding the alarm of the soon coming of King Jesus Christ.